TASTE the LITTLE KAROO

Beate Joubert

TASTE the LITTLE KAROO

Beate Joubert

Dedication

For Meyer; my daughters Hannah Katerien, Julia Heleen and Lena Beate;

my son Andreas Meyer De la Courtte; my parents; and my sisters Carmen, Catanja and Varenka

Acknowledgements

My grateful thanks to Linda de Villiers and the entire team at Penguin Random House South Africa.

Also to Errieda du Toit, Sonja Cabano, Carmen Niehaus, Sumien Brink, Adriaan Oosthuizen, Andries Dreyer Joubert, Helen Henn, Samarie Smith, as well as so many others who have inspired Meyer and me.

First published in hardcover in 2015 by Struik Lifestyle (an imprint of Penguin Random House South Africa (Pty) Ltd)
Company Reg. No. 1953/000441/07
The Estuaries, 4 Oxbow Crescent, Century Avenue, Century City 7441
PO Box 1144, Cape Town, 8000, South Africa
www.penguinrandomhouse.co.za

This edition published in 2016

Reprinted in 2017

PUBLISHER: Linda de Villiers
DESIGN MANAGER: Beverley Dodd
DESIGNER: Helen Henn
EDITOR: Anja Grobler
TRANSLATOR: Thea Grobbelaar
PROOFREADER: Gill Gordon
PHOTOGRAPHERS: Sean Calitz, Matthys van Lill and Andries Joubert (for detailed credits, see photographic credits below)
FOOD STYLIST: Brita du Plessis
FOOD STYLIST'S ASSISTANT: Elizabeth Ingram

Reproduction: Hirt & Carter Cape (Pty) Ltd
Printing and binding: RR Donnelley Asia Printing Solutions Ltd, China

ISBN 978-1-43230-794-3

Photographic credits:

All images by Sean Calitz; except for Matthys van Lill (cover, end papers and spine) and Andries Joubert (pages 8–9, 19, 20, 23, 24 (left), 28 (all), 34–35, 36–37 (all), 40–41 (all), 42–43, 45 (right), 55, 59 (all), 60, 62–63, 71 (left and top right), 73, 89 (all), 93 (right), 96, 97, 102 (right), 103, 108 (right), 110, 113 (left), 117 (all), 121 (all), 124–125, 129 (left), 131 (all), 136, 139, 144 (all), 150 (all), 152–153, 164 (all), 165, 166–167, 169 (top), 170, 174, 175, 178, 179, 183 (all), 184-185)

Contents

Introduction

It fills me with immense pride to present the Little Karoo – in its many and unique facets – for you to 'taste', whether in the authentic dishes (including healthy and modern Mediterranean-inspired combinations), wine, atmosphere or lifestyle.

Our farm, Joubert-Tradauw, along with the Alfresco Deli and wine cellar, is situated in the Tradouw Valley near Barrydale, on the R62 route. The area is well known for its high quality fruit, vineyards, small game, ostriches and unique fynbos vegetation.

Many years ago, while living and working in California, Scotland, Switzerland and other parts of Europe, I was inspired mostly by the culinary traditions of the French and Spanish, and their Mediterranean, earthy foods: great breads, olive oil, spreads, herbs and fresh salads.

In my kitchen, I love to experiment with ideas and ingredients – from Little Karoo 'boere tapas' to be eaten al fresco, to traditional dishes with a Mediterranean twist. Old favourites are given a makeover, yet retain their authentic Little Karoo roots and names.

Taste the Little Karoo is a celebration of the good life, where the focus of meals is fresh, seasonal and simple, but tasty so that every flavour, aroma and ingredient becomes a new discovery. Meals are special occasions, and that Karoo spirit of sharing is one of the most important elements in my motivation for establishing the Alfresco Deli.

This is therefore far more than a mere cookbook. I hope it will serve as an inspiration for home cooks and entertainers, wine lovers and lifestyle enthusiasts to try out new ideas and taste sensations. I've included a wine list using wines from the region that will perfectly complement the food. Add to that original table linen and beautiful crockery and cutlery, and you will begin to understand the charm of the Little Karoo.

I appreciate everyone who has had a positive influence on, and been an inspiration in, my food journey. To those I don't know personally or may unwittingly have left out, I give you my thanks as well in helping me to 'colour' my book.

Be brave, play with ingredients and flavours, and most of all, taste the Little Karoo!

TRADOUW
PASS • PAS

This pass was constructed by Masterbuilder
Thomas Bain between 1869 and 1873.

Hierdie pas is ontwerp en gebou deur die Meester
pasbouer Thomas Bain tussen 1869 en 1873.

Tradouw is a Khoi'san word meaning "the women's
poort / path."

Tradouw is 'n Khoisan woord wat "die vroue se
poort / pad" beteken.

Tapas

My aim is to provide an alfresco dining experience of inspiring and mouth-watering foods and taste sensations at the Alfresco Deli in the heart of the Tradouw Valley. Authentic Little Karoo ingredients and dishes become '*boere tapas*' and are presented Mediterranean style, to create something novel in the combination of traditional and modern. As with the people of the French countryside, we in the Little Karoo prefer an uncomplicated lifestyle, one that focuses on flavours that are satisfying and true, allowing each bite to tell a story.

Camembert parcel with a berry sauce

Serves 4–6

10-cm Camembert round
6 preserved green figs, thinly
    sliced (reserve the syrup)
¼ cup roasted almond flakes
4 sheets phyllo pastry
melted butter

Berry sauce
1 cup mixed berries and
    strawberries
¼ cup castor sugar
¼ cup reserved fig syrup (see
    above) or verjuice

To prepare the cheese parcel*, slice the Camembert in half horizontally. Place one half on a plate and arrange half of the fig slices and almonds on top, then cover it with the other half.

Preheat the oven to 150 °C.

Cut three sheets of phyllo pastry into neat, large squares that will fit easily around the cheese stack. Brush each sheet with the melted butter. Layer the sheets on top of each other, then place the cheese stack in the centre of the layered sheets. Arrange the remaining figs and almonds on top of the stack and wrap the phyllo sheets around the ingredients to create a parcel. Scrunch the remaining sheet of phyllo and place it on top of the parcel. Brush with the melted butter.

Bake on the middle shelf of the oven until the pastry is light brown and the cheese starts to melt.

For the berry sauce, heat the mixed berries, castor sugar and fig syrup or verjuice in a saucepan, stirring until the berries are soft and the mixture becomes syrupy. As soon as you take the cheese parcel out of the oven, drizzle the berry sauce over it, and serve immediately.

* If you like, you may omit the phyllo pastry entirely and simply serve as an open stack, as pictured.

Delicious to eat under the trees on a summer day with freshly baked ciabatta.

Cheesy chicken Kiev

Serves 6–8

2 Tbsp soft butter
230-g tub smooth
    cottage cheese (plain or
    with spring onions)
1 tsp grated lemon rind
2 tsp freshly squeezed
    lemon juice
3 cloves garlic, peeled and
    finely chopped
2 Tbsp chicken spice
2 tsp Thai spice
⅓ cup finely chopped fresh
    flat-leaf parsley
2 tsp very finely sliced
    Peppadews,
salt and black pepper to taste
8 skinless and boneless
    chicken breasts, washed
    and dried

Crust

3 Tbsp cake flour
1 Tbsp chicken spice
1 egg, beaten
± 2 cups fine white
    breadcrumbs

Mix the butter, cottage cheese, lemon rind and juice, garlic, chicken and Thai spices, parsley, Peppadews, and salt and pepper until combined. Spoon the mixture into a plastic bag, roll it up into a tube measuring 4 cm in diameter and place in the freezer until firm.

Place the chicken fillets on a flat surface and slice in half horizontally. Flatten each piece with a rolling pin. Slice the frozen butter roll into 16 circles. Place a circle onto one end of each fillet and roll up the fillet from this end. Secure with a toothpick. Repeat the process until all the fillets have been rolled up.

Preheat the oven to 180 °C. To make the crust, mix the flour with the chicken spice. Dip the fillets in the flour mixture, then in the beaten egg, followed by the breadcrumbs. Arrange on a baking tray and refrigerate for 30 minutes. Cover loosely with aluminium foil and bake for 15 minutes. Remove the foil, return to the oven and bake until golden-brown.

Serve with vegetables and a salad, or as a tapas snack.

Inspired by Shanaaz Parker

Makes 6–8 small bowls of each

Lamb kidneys
500 g lamb kidneys, washed
3 Tbsp canola oil
2½ Tbsp butter
1 large red onion, finely chopped
2 tsp chopped fresh thyme
2 cups thinly sliced button mushrooms
1 Tbsp chopped sweet red pepper
1 tsp coarse salt
2 cloves garlic, crushed
1 tsp dried thyme
1 tsp paprika
½ tsp cayenne pepper
1 cup red wine
1 tsp cornflour mixed with a little water to form a paste
a handful of chopped fresh parsley

Chicken livers
3 Tbsp butter (or more)
2 Tbsp olive oil for frying
500 g chicken livers, washed
1 shallot, peeled and finely chopped
1 onion, peeled and sliced into thin rings
1 tsp coarse salt
2 tsp finely chopped garlic
1 Tbsp chopped sweet green pepper
1 tsp chopped fresh rosemary
1½ tsp mixed dried herbs
½ tsp white pepper
1 cup dry white wine
2 Tbsp port or brandy
½ cup fresh cream
toasted sesame seeds for garnishing
freshly ground black pepper
chopped fresh parsley
onion marmalade for serving

Lamb kidneys and chicken livers

For the lamb kidneys
Cut the kidneys in half lengthwise and remove any membranes and most of the veins. Rinse the kidneys in a little salted water, then drain. Cut each half into half again. Heat the canola oil in a pan and fry the kidneys until light brown, then remove from the pan. Do not overcook.

Melt the butter in the same pan and fry the onion, fresh thyme, mushrooms and red pepper with the salt until the onions are light brown. Add the garlic and cook for a minute. Add the kidneys and stir until coated with the onion mixture. Add the dried thyme, paprika and cayenne pepper. Slowly pour in the red wine and check the consistency of the sauce; if it is too dry, add more wine or water. Cook until everything is just combined, but the kidneys should still be light pink inside. When the sauce has reduced a little, remove the pan from the stove-top and stir in the cornflour mixture. Return the pan to the stove-top and leave to simmer until the sauce thickens.

Spoon into small bowls and sprinkle with the parsley. Serve with slices of toasted olive ciabatta (see page 55).

For the chicken livers
Heat the butter and olive oil in a pan over medium to high heat, then flash-fry the livers until just sealed. Remove from the pan. Sauté the shallot, onion, salt, garlic, green pepper and rosemary until the shallot and onion slices are soft. Return the livers to the pan with the dried herbs, pepper and white wine and port or brandy. Flambé the mixture and when the flames have died down, add the cream and stir through. Cook until the livers are soft, but still light pink inside.

Spoon into bowls and sprinkle over sesame seeds, black pepper and chopped parsley. Serve with slices of toasted molasses bread (see page 56) and onion marmalade.

Pastry shells

1 cup cake flour
½ tsp salt
1 Tbsp finely chopped
   fresh thyme
50 g cold butter, grated
¼ cup water

Filling

½ cup crumbled feta
3 ripe figs, sliced
3 large eggs, separated
1 tsp finely chopped
   spring onions
½ cup crème fraîche
⅓ cup Bulgarian yoghurt
½ cup chopped walnuts, plus
   extra for garnishing
salt to taste
a pinch of white pepper
thin strips of coppa or Parma
   ham to taste
fresh micro herbs for
   garnishing
toasted sesame seeds
   for garnishing
ripe figs, halved for
   garnishing
balsamic reduction
   for drizzling
freshly ground black pepper
   to taste

Crème fraîche tartlets with figs and thyme

For the pastry shells

Grease six 8-cm ramekins with butter.

Combine the flour, salt and thyme in a bowl. Using your fingertips, rub the grated butter into the flour mixture until it resembles breadcrumbs. Add the water gradually and mix until a dough is formed. Cover with clingfilm and refrigerate until chilled.

On a lightly floured surface, roll out the pastry. Press out circles that are large enough to line the ramekins with 2 cm of overhanging pastry. Line the ramekins with the pastry and prick the bases of the pastry shells with a fork. Refrigerate for 30 minutes.

Preheat the oven to 180 °C. Blind bake the shells for 15 minutes or until just light brown. Remove the ramekins from the oven and set aside. Leave the oven on, to bake the filling.

For the filling

Divide the feta and figs among the pastry shells. Mix together the egg yolks, spring onions, crème fraîche, yoghurt, nuts and seasoning until combined. Whisk the egg whites until stiff peaks form, then fold into the yoghurt mixture and spoon into the pastry shells.

Arrange the strips of coppa or Parma ham on top and bake for about 25 minutes until golden-brown. Remove from the oven and allow to cool. Garnish with the micro herbs, sesame seeds, walnuts and fig halves, then drizzle over some balsamic reduction and add a grinding of black pepper.

Makes 18

Chickpea balls

410-g can chickpeas, drained
410-g can whole kernel corn,
   or the same amount cut
   from cooked mealies
8 finely chopped spring
   onions
½ cup finely chopped fresh
   flat-leaf parsley
2 tsp crushed garlic
a few strips finely sliced
   anchovy to taste
1 Tbsp finely chopped sweet
   red pepper
1 tsp turmeric
1 tsp paprika
1 tsp prepared English
   mustard
1 Tbsp hot peach chutney
salt to taste

Crumbs

cake flour (enough to cover
   the balls)
butter or non-stick cooking
   spray
2–3 eggs or more as
   needed, whisked
fine white breadcrumbs
   (enough to cover the balls)
canola oil

Topping

125 g smooth cottage cheese
1 Tbsp prepared hot English
   mustard
1 tsp paprika
2 Tbsp finely chopped fresh
   flat-leaf parsley
6 finely chopped spring onions
onion marmalade to taste
freshly ground black pepper
   to taste

Chickpea, cottage cheese and spring onion balls

For the balls

Place all the ingredients for the balls into a food processor and process until smooth. Using your hands, shape the mixture into balls, then flatten them ever-so-slightly.

For the crumbs

Roll the balls lightly in flour and refrigerate for 1 hour. Preheat the oven to 200 °C. Grease a baking tray with butter or spray with cooking spray.

Dip the balls into the whisked egg, then coat them in the breadcrumbs. Arrange them on the prepared baking tray, spaced slightly apart, brush with oil and bake for 5 minutes.

For the topping

Combine the cottage cheese, mustard, paprika and parsley. Arrange the baked balls on a large platter with a teaspoon of the cottage cheese topping spooned over each. Sprinkle the spring onions over them, then top each with onion marmalade and a grinding of black pepper.

I serve these on tapas platters with fresh bread, or in a salad as an appetiser — healthy and delicious!

Easy oven-baked frittata

Serves 4–6

2 Tbsp olive oil
6 thinly sliced spring onions
6 thinly sliced courgettes
1 sweet red pepper, diced
salt and freshly ground black
　　pepper to taste
¼ cup grated Gruyère cheese
½ cup pitted black
　　olives, halved
6 large eggs, beaten
6 medium red-skinned
　　potatoes, peeled
a handful of fresh watercress
extra shavings of Gruyère
　　for garnishing

Preheat the oven to 200 °C.

Pour the olive oil into a 20–25-cm ovenproof dish and add the spring onions, courgettes and red pepper to the dish. Season with the salt and pepper and roast for 10 minutes.

Combine the grated cheese and olives with the eggs. Remove the dish from the oven and pour the egg mixture over the vegetables. Mix everything together well, then bake for about 20 minutes or until the egg has set.

Boil the potatoes until soft, then drain and slice. Slice the frittata. Place a slice of hot potato onto a slice of frittata and cover with another slice of frittata. Garnish with watercress and shavings of Gruyère. Serve with a really hot chilli sauce for the brave.

On Sunday mornings I often make a tasty frittata for my children. Sometimes they miss breakfast and have it as a starter while they wait for lunch. Alternatively, I serve it as a side dish, or sliced as a brunch dish.

Serves 4–6

3 large sweet red peppers
2 large brinjals, thinly sliced
　into rounds
olive oil
coarse or smoked salt to taste
6 courgettes, each sliced
　lengthwise into 6 strips
± 10 thin slices of strong
　white cheese e.g. Edam
　or Cheddar
2 rounds feta, crumbled
½ cup chopped fresh flat-leaf
　parsley for garnishing
freshly ground pepper
grated Parmesan to taste
fresh coriander leaves
　for garnishing
1 tsp white pepper

Tomato sauce

2 large onions, peeled and
　roughly chopped
4 cloves garlic, peeled and
　finely chopped
½ tsp salt
¼ cup olive oil
15 small ripe tomatoes,
　plunged into boiling water
　and skinned
10 black olives, pitted
　and halved
2 Tbsp balsamic or red
　grape vinegar
¼ cup white sugar
½ tsp freshly ground
　black pepper
1 Tbsp Tabasco sauce
½ tsp chilli flakes (optional)
¼ cup finely chopped sweet
　red or green peppers

Terrine with brinjal and red peppers

Preheat the oven grill.

Arrange the red peppers in an ovenproof dish and grill until almost scorched. While still hot, transfer them to a plastic bag to sweat for about 20 minutes. Remove the skin and pith, then dice and set aside.

Add the brinjal slices to the same roasting dish, brush both sides with oil and sprinkle with salt. Grill for about 4 minutes on each side until soft and browned. Remove and set aside.

Add the courgette strips to the same dish, brush with olive oil and grill in the oven until soft.

To assemble the terrine, line a 22 x 12-cm baking dish with thick plastic or aluminium foil. Beginning with the brinjal, arrange slices in the bottom of the dish, followed by a third each of the red peppers, courgettes and cheeses. Continue layering in this fashion, ending with a layer of brinjal.

Pour boiling water over the parsley, then immediately remove and plunge in ice cold water, and drain. Sprinkle the parsley and season with salt and pepper over the top of the terrine. Cover the terrine with a layer of plastic or foil and press down firmly and slowly to compact the mixture. Allow to cool at room temperature, then refrigerate until required.

To make the tomato sauce, sauté the onions, garlic and salt in the olive oil until glossy. Add the remaining ingredients and cook until reduced by half and quite thick.

Slice the terrine. Spoon the tomato sauce onto a serving dish and arrange the terrine slices on the sauce. Garnish with the Parmesan and coriander leaves, and sprinkle over the pepper.

Presentation is important with this terrine; serve the slices on a beautiful platter.

Serves 4

250 g fresh baby artichokes
  or 410-g can artichokes,
  drained
lemon juice (if necessary)
olive oil to taste
2 Tbsp butter
1 cup thinly sliced prosciutto
  or Parma ham
2 tsp finely chopped garlic
1 Tbsp chopped fresh sage
¾ cup kalamata olives, pitted
  and quartered
¼ cup fresh lemon juice
3 Tbsp chopped fresh parsley
½ tsp dried chilli flakes
½ cup fresh cream
2 x tagliatelle (see page 187)
2 egg yolks
Ina Paarman's Seasoned Sea
  Salt to taste
freshly ground black pepper
  to taste
½ cup grated pecorino,
  Gruyère or Parmesan
1 Tbsp basil pesto (optional)
cheese shavings (your choice)
  for garnishing

Tagliatelle with artichokes

If using fresh artichokes, remove the outer leaves and discard, then chop up the remaining artichokes. Soak in a mixture of water and lemon juice (drain before cooking).

Heat the olive oil in a pan and fry the artichokes for 2–3 minutes on each side until golden-brown. Add the butter and prosciutto or Parma ham, garlic and sage and stir through. Fry for 1–2 minutes, then remove from the heat. Stir in the olives, fresh lemon juice, parsley, chilli flakes and cream.

Boil the tagliatelle in salted water until *al dente*. Remove from the heat and immediately stir through the egg yolks, salt, pepper, cheese and pesto (if using). Serve the pasta with the sauce over it with pepper, olive oil and cheese shavings of your choice.

Wild mushroom and coppa tagliatelle with truffle oil

Serves 6

2 red onions, peeled and
    finely sliced into rings
2 tsp Maldon salt
2 cloves garlic, peeled
    and crushed
1 sweet red pepper, diced
5 each fresh wild, oyster and
    brown mushrooms
4 dried mushrooms, soaked
    in hot water until soft
    then sliced
2 tsp mushroom powder
    (see Tips) or a ready-
    made mushroom stock
    concentrate
1 cup chicken stock
1 cup fresh cream
1 egg yolk
3 Tbsp good-quality truffle oil
cooked tagliatelle (see page
    187) (make as much as
    you require)
12 thin slices coppa ham
fresh rocket leaves
toasted sesame seeds
    for sprinkling
½ cup grated Parmesan
black pepper to taste

Sauté the onions, salt, garlic, red pepper and fresh and dried mushrooms until golden-brown. Add the mushroom powder, chicken stock and warm water in which the mushrooms were soaked, then simmer until the mixture thickens. Stir through the cream and allow the mixture to reduce to the desired consistency.

Stir the egg yolk and the truffle oil through the cooked tagliatelle. Spoon the sauce over the pasta. Garnish with the slices of coppa ham and rocket leaves. Sprinkle over the sesame seeds and Parmesan, and grind over some black pepper.

TIPS: Adding a truffle flavour to a homemade pasta gives it an amazing boost. Always keep a good-quality truffle oil in stock, and add it to any dish – it's a winner!

If you want to make your own mushroom powder, simply buy dried mushrooms (or leave fresh, thinly sliced mushrooms in a sheltered area outside to dry out) and grind them into a fine powder. The powder is quite concentrated and you need only use 1 or 2 teaspoons of it for a delicious mushroom flavour.

This is my ideal lunch for a lazy Saturday under the trees in the heavenly Tradouw Valley, with a glass of chilled Joubert-Tradauw Chardonnay. I dedicate the recipe to my chef friends Anna who owns La Campanola and Luca who owns Luca's in Johannesburg.

Serves 12

Pastry
½ cup butter
1 cup cake flour
a pinch of salt
1 tsp baking powder
½ cup finely grated strong
    white Cheddar cheese
1 egg
a few drops of ice cold water
    (if needed)

Filling
250 g bacon, finely chopped
2 Tbsp cake flour
1½ cups thick fresh cream
230-g tub smooth cottage
    cheese
4 large eggs, beaten
salt and black pepper to taste
½ tsp grated nutmeg
1 cup grated strong Dutch
    cheese of your choice
1 Tbsp butter
15 thin slices coppa or Parma
    ham for garnishing
a handful of fresh rocket
    leaves
Gruyère shavings for
    garnishing
freshly ground black pepper

Beate's quiche Lorraine

For the pastry
Grease a loose-bottomed 20-cm diameter fluted flan dish or a rectangular 22 x 18-cm flan dish.

First mix, then knead (by hand or in a mixer), all the ingredients until they come together to form a soft dough. If the mixture is too dry, add a few drops of water. Roll the dough out on a lightly floured surface, then line the base and sides of the dish with the dough. Trim away any excess bits, to neaten. Refrigerate until the filling is ready.

For the filling
Preheat the oven to 180 °C.

Fry the bacon lightly and add to the base of the pastry shell. Mix the flour with a little cream, then combine this mixture with the cottage cheese. Mix together the remaining cream, cottage cheese mixture, eggs, salt, pepper, nutmeg and cheese, then pour the mixture over the bacon in the pastry shell. Dot with butter and bake for 50 minutes until lightly browned and set.

Garnish with the ham, rocket leaves, Gruyère shavings and a grinding of pepper.

A classic quiche is always popular, and this one is no exception.

Spanakopita tart

Serves 12

2 medium onions, peeled
  and chopped
2 medium red onions, peeled
  and sliced into rings
4 cloves garlic, peeled
  and chopped
2–3 Tbsp butter
125 g chopped coppa or
  bacon (optional)
40 raw spinach leaves,
  stalks removed
4 rounds feta, roughly
  crumbled
1 Tbsp toasted pine nuts
20 sheets phyllo pastry
melted butter
toasted sesame seeds
  for sprinkling

Preheat the oven to 180 °C. Grease a 30 x 20-cm casserole dish, about 6 cm deep.

Sauté the onions and garlic in the butter over medium heat until transparent, then add the coppa or bacon, if using.

Steam the spinach until just wilted, then chop finely. Stir in the feta while the spinach is still hot. Combine the onion mixture with the spinach mixture and the pine nuts.

Brush about 12 of the phyllo sheets with the melted butter, then use them to line the bottom of the prepared casserole dish. Spoon over the filling and cover with the remaining sheets of phyllo, also brushed with the butter. (I usually crumple the last 3 or 4 sheets for decoration.)

Sprinkle the sesame seeds over the top and bake for about 25 minutes or until golden-brown.

Cut the tart into squares before serving.

Sweetcorn triangles

Makes 12–16

4 Tbsp canola oil

3 red onions, peeled and sliced

2 cloves garlic, peeled
and chopped

coarse salt to taste

1 small piece fresh ginger,
grated

1 green chilli, seeded and
finely chopped

1 jalapeño chilli, chopped

2 Tbsp chopped sweet
red pepper

1 tsp paprika

1 tsp cayenne pepper

½ x 410-g can cream-style
sweetcorn

½ x 410-g can whole
kernel corn

2 Tbsp lemon juice

zest of 1 lemon

500-g packet phyllo pastry

1 Tbsp butter, melted

2 Tbsp dry-fried and finely
chopped almonds

1 bunch fresh coriander leaves

toasted sesame seeds
for sprinkling

Preheat the oven to 200 °C. Grease a baking tray.

Heat the oil and fry the onions, garlic and salt until golden-brown. Add the ginger, chillies, red pepper, paprika and cayenne pepper, and stir through. Mix in both types of corn and the lemon juice and zest until combined.

Stack three sheets of phyllo on top of one another, brushing each sheet well with the melted butter right to the edges of the pastry. Cut each stack into 4 long strips, each about 6 cm in width. Spoon a tablespoon of filling onto the centre of each strip. Sprinkle some almonds over the top of each.

Fold the strips into triangles, beginning at one end. Repeat the process with the remaining phyllo sheets. Seal each tringle with a little oil and arrange them on the prepared baking tray. Bake for 5–10 minutes on the middle rack of the oven, or until golden-brown. Sprinkle the triangles with the coriander and sesame seeds.

This is what I would make for a knockout round in a cooking competition.

1 cup cake flour
1 Tbsp fine coconut or
   almond flour (available
   from health shops)
1 cup mealie meal
1 cup uncooked polenta
1 tsp salt
4 tsp baking powder
1 courgette, grated
1 carrot, finely grated
½ sweet green pepper,
   finely chopped
1 Tbsp chopped fresh basil
1 Tbsp chopped fresh parsley
1 Tbsp chopped fresh
   coriander leaves
1 Tbsp dried mixed herbs
1 tsp ground cumin
1 cup beer or soda water
410-g can whole kernel corn,
   or the same amount cut
   from cooked mealies
canola oil for frying
150 g Camembert, cut into
   12 pieces
freshly ground black pepper
250 g streaky bacon, fried
   until crispy
golden syrup for dipping

Mealie fritters with bacon and Camembert

Combine the flours, mealie meal, polenta, salt, baking powder, courgette, carrot, green pepper, herbs and cumin. Gradually add the beer or soda water, until mixed through. If the batter is too dry, add a little water, then stir in the corn.

Heat some oil in a frying pan, then drop spoonfuls of the batter into the pan, leaving space for spreading. When bubbles start to form at the top, flip the fritters over with a spatula and fry for another 1–2 minutes until golden-brown. Remove from the pan and drain on paper towel. Keep warm.

Place a piece of Camembert on each fritter and allow to melt until creamy. Grind over lots of black pepper. Serve with rashers of bacon and golden syrup in a dipping bowl.

Carmen's classic cheese soufflé

Serves 12

½ cup butter
½ cup cake flour
2 cups milk (plus extra
   if necessary)
6 eggs, separated
1½ tsp salt
a pinch of cayenne pepper
2 tsp mustard powder
1 cup grated Gruyère
1 cup grated strong white
   Cheddar or Dutch cheese
a little grated nutmeg
extra grated Gruyère
   (optional)

Preheat the oven to 200 °C.

Make a white sauce by melting the butter in a pan and stirring in the flour until the mixture starts to colour. Gradually add the milk while whisking until the mixture thickens and becomes a smooth, thick sauce. Remove from the heat, beat the egg yolks and stir into the sauce. Add the salt, pepper and mustard powder. Beat the egg whites until stiff peaks form, then fold into the sauce. Finally fold in the cheeses.

Pour the mixture into an ungreased ovenproof bowl. Place the bowl in a roasting dish with boiling water that reaches halfway up the sides of the bowl. Bake for 8 minutes then reduce the heat to 180 °C and bake for another 40–45 minutes until set and light brown.

Remove from the oven and serve immediately. Sprinkle with grated nutmeg and extra Gruyère on the side (if using).

A delicious French cheese soufflé may be served as a starter, a main course with fresh bread, a side dish, or as part of a tapas platter.

Serves 8–10

4 whole tomatoes
4 red onions, peeled and
    quartered
4 onions, peeled and
    thickly sliced
1 tsp Maldon salt
1 sweet red pepper, pith
    removed and quartered
1 sweet green pepper, pith
    removed and quartered
1 red chilli, finely chopped
1 green chilli, finely chopped
4 cloves garlic, peeled and
    roughly chopped
a sprig of fresh rosemary,
    finely chopped
a sprig of fresh thyme,
    finely chopped
¼ cup olive oil
1 cup chardonnay wine
1 cup cold vegetable or
    meat stock
410-g can tomato-and-
    onion mix
1 cup pitted and halved
    black olives
10 thick slices brinjal,
    chopped
6–8 courgettes, thickly sliced
    on the diagonal
1 tsp white pepper
freshly ground black pepper
    to taste
finely chopped fresh
    coriander for garnishing

Ratatouille on polenta

Place the tomatoes in a bowl and pour over boiling water. Remove from the water, skin and cut into quarters.

In a saucepan, fry the onions, salt, peppers, chillies, garlic and herbs in the olive oil over a medium heat until soft. Add the wine and stock, followed by the tomato quarters, tomato-and-onion mix, olives and brinjal. Simmer, covered, over a low heat for approximately 30 minutes. Add the courgettes and continue to simmer, uncovered, until the sauce has thickened and the vegetables are soft but not disintegrating. Season with the white and black pepper, but do not stir again until ready to serve. Garnish with the coriander.

TIP: Serve on a bed of soft polenta (about 3–4 cups, made according to the packet instructions). You can also make a firm polenta, which can be shaped into fingers and fried in a griddle pan to give them a striped appearance. Alternatively, roll the polenta into balls and deep-fry them in oil.

I often serve this with pork, or as a side dish with any meat, or even on its own for vegetarians.

Wild mushroom risotto in white wine

Serves 12

½ cup dried porcini
   mushrooms
6 cups hot chicken or
   vegetable stock
3 Tbsp butter for frying
1 cup chopped button
   mushrooms
1 cup chopped brown
   mushrooms
olive oil to taste
2 onions, peeled and
   finely chopped
2 celery stalks, finely chopped
1 Tbsp chopped fresh thyme
coarse sea salt to taste
freshly ground black pepper
400 g uncooked arborio rice
1 cup chardonnay or dry
   white wine
1 cup sliced oyster mushrooms
1 cup sliced fresh porcini
   mushrooms (if available)
a few sprigs fresh parsley,
   finely chopped
1 cup grated Parmesan,
   pecorino or Gruyère
lemon juice for drizzling
steamed baby asparagus
   spears for garnishing
½ cup toasted almond flakes
   for garnishing

Soak the dried mushrooms in a bowl with just enough hot chicken or vegetable stock (about 1 cup) to cover them, until they are soft. Remove the mushrooms from the stock and set the stock aside. Melt 2 tablespoons of the butter in a pan and fry the button and brown mushrooms until they are just soft. Remove from the pan and set aside.

Add the olive oil to a 30-cm wok and sauté the onions, celery and thyme with a little of salt and pepper for about 10 minutes, ensuring that the onion doesn't change colour. Increase the heat and add the rice while stirring continuously. Gradually pour in the wine, still stirring, and cook until the wine has been absorbed by the rice. Stir in the button, brown and porcini mushrooms.

Add 1 cup of the stock in which the mushrooms were soaked, as well as 1 cup of the chicken or vegetable stock. Reduce the heat and add the remaining stock (but reserve a little for later, if necessary), a little at a time, allowing each amount to be absorbed by the rice before adding more. Cook until the rice is *al dente*. This will take about 30 minutes.

Fry the oyster and fresh porcini mushrooms in the previously used pan until soft. Transfer to a bowl, then add the parsley and season with a pinch of salt and pepper to taste.

Stir the remaining butter and half of the Parmesan, pecorino or Gruyère through the risotto. The risotto must be creamy so add more stock, if necessary.

Spoon a generous helping of risotto onto each plate with a portion of the fried oyster and fresh porcini mushrooms. Drizzle with olive oil, a little lemon juice and sprinkle over the remaining grated cheese, and a grinding of black pepper if preferred. Garnish each plate with a spear of asparagus and some almond flakes.

A good risotto really does it for me! Make your own stock – you will definitely taste the difference.

Tasty polenta tart

Makes 1 medium tart

4 cups boiling water
2 tsp salt
2 cups uncooked polenta
1 tsp cumin seeds
½ tsp cayenne pepper
½ tsp paprika
filling (see Tip)
2 Tbsp butter, melted
freshly ground black pepper
  to taste (optional)
fresh herbs for garnishing
  (optional)
balsamic reduction for
  drizzling (optional)

Preheat the oven to 180 °C. Line a roasting pan or casserole dish with baking paper so that the paper protrudes a little beyond the edges of the pan or dish (to make it easier to lift the tart out of the pan).

Bring the water and salt to the boil, then gradually sprinkle the polenta over the boiling water. Stir in the cumin seeds, cayenne pepper and paprika. Cook, stirring occasionally, until the polenta is ready (15–20 minutes), but be careful as the polenta can burn easily.

Press half of the polenta into the base of the pan or dish. Pack a layer of the filling of your choice over the polenta, then press the remaining polenta over the filling. Brush the melted butter over the top and bake for 20 minutes. Leave it to cool, then refrigerate for about 1 hour to set.

Reheat before serving. Serve with lots of black pepper, fresh herbs of your choice and a splash of balsamic reduction.

TIP: The following are just some ideas for a filling, but the list is endless: slices of roasted brinjal, sliced and roasted sweet green or red peppers, whole roasted cloves of garlic, thin shavings of Parmesan, chopped chillies, pitted olives, tapenade, chopped fresh coriander or basil, pesto.

I use polenta for this delicious tart, but mealie meal works just as well. It looks great if you slice it and arrange it on a large serving dish, or serve it with a 'potjiekos'.

Roulade wheels with filling

Makes ± 10

3 Tbsp butter
½ cup cake flour
2 cups milk
4 eggs, separated
a pinch of salt
garlic salt to taste

Fillings (your choice)

230-g tub spring onion or
    Peppadew cream cheese
¼ cup biltong powder
freshly ground black pepper
    to taste

2 Tbsp olive tapenade
chopped fresh red chilli
    to taste
¼ cup green pesto

230-g tub plain smooth
    cream cheese
¼ cup roasted, peeled and
    chopped sweet red pepper
capers to taste

Line a deep, 40 x 25-cm rectangular baking dish with baking or wax paper that's been greased with butter or sprayed with non-stick cooking spray. Preheat the oven to 160 °C.

Melt the butter in a saucepan over medium heat and whisk in the flour until it becomes a smooth paste. Pour in the milk and continue whisking into a smooth, thick sauce. Whisk the egg yolks into the white sauce.

In a separate bowl, beat the egg whites until stiff, then fold into the white sauce. Season to taste with salt and garlic salt.

Transfer the mixture to the prepared baking dish and bake for about 40 minutes until golden-brown and firm to the touch.

Grease or spray another sheet of baking or wax paper. Turn out the roulade onto the prepared paper. Carefully remove the paper from the original base and leave the roulade to cool. Spread the surface with a filling of your choice (see ideas below), leaving a 4-cm border clear. Roll up – Swiss roll style – removing the second sheet of paper as you go. Wrap the roll in foil and chill. Slice the roll into 3 cm-thick slices before serving.

Filling suggestions

* Mix together the spring onion or Peppadew cream cheese, biltong powder and black pepper.
* Mix together the olive tapenade, chillies and pesto.
* Mix together the plain cream cheese, roasted red pepper and capers.

These snacks are so simple and creative, and can be delicate or fiery in flavour.

Grandma Katy's brawn

Makes 1 large brawn

12 sheep's trotters
4 pig's trotters
1 cup lime juice, diluted in
 9 litres boiling water
1 sheep's stomach
4 cups fresh water
2 tsp salt
1 tsp white pepper
3 Tbsp canola oil
3 medium onions, sliced
2 Tbsp hot curry powder
1 Tbsp turmeric
a few threads of saffron
1 cup balsamic or grape
 vinegar
juice of 2 lemons
1 tsp ground coriander
2 Tbsp apricot jam or
 peach chutney
4 cloves garlic, peeled
12 allspice
1 tsp whole cloves
12 black peppercorns
1 Tbsp coriander seeds
4 bay leaves

Soak all the trotters in the hot lime water mixture for a day, then scrape them clean. Discard the water. Soak the trotters and stomach in salted water (they must be submerged in the water) for 2 hours then drain. Cut the trotters into small pieces and the stomach into strips. Discard the salted water. Cover with 8 cups fresh water in a pressure cooker, add the salt and pepper and cook over a low heat for about 50 minutes or until soft. Add more water if necessary. Remove the meat from the pressure cooker and leave to cool down, but reserve the cooking liquid.

Heat the oil in a saucepan and sauté the onions until soft, then stir in the curry powder, turmeric and saffron.

Cut the cooled meat off the bones and discard the bones. Return the meat to the pressure cooker, along with the reserved cooking liquid, curried onions, balsamic or grape vinegar, lemon juice, ground coriander, apricot jam or peach chutney and garlic. Season with more salt and pepper if necessary. Place the allspice, whole cloves, black peppercorns, coriander seeds and bay leaves in a muslin bag, and add to the pressure cooker. Cook for about 1 hour. Remove the muslin bag and allow the mixture to cool.

Grease a 3-litre glass loaf dish and line with clingfilm. Pour the mixture into the dish and refrigerate until set. It will keep in the fridge for up to two weeks. Turn out the brawn and slice thinly. Serve with fresh bread and a salad.

I love a good brawn. My grandma from Sutherland used to make it for us when we visited the farm Klipbanksrivier and I always enjoyed helping her.

This is Meyer's favourite recipe, best prepared in a frying pan. The bones have a unique flavour.

Serves 4

12 beef marrowbones with marrow and a bit of meat on the bones
1 Tbsp olive oil or to taste
½ tsp coarse salt
2 tsp chopped fresh rosemary
1 Tbsp butter
freshly ground black pepper to taste
½ tsp paprika
½ tsp cayenne pepper
¼ cup brandy (optional)

Pan-fried marrowbones

Fry the marrowbones in a deep frying pan with the olive oil until both sides are golden-brown. Season with coarse salt and sprinkle over the rosemary. Add the butter and fry until the rosemary is soft. Add the black pepper, paprika and cayenne pepper. Pour in the brandy (if using) and simmer lightly, uncovered, until the meat is tender.

Serve hot with with toasted ciabatta and another grinding of black pepper.

Krister's salt-roasted potatoes with tarragon sauce

Serves 15

1 kg unpeeled red and brown new potatoes, rinsed
⅓ cup olive oil
1 Tbsp Maldon salt
6 cloves garlic, peeled and crushed
1 Tbsp chopped fresh rosemary
1 whole garlic bulb, unpeeled (optional)

Tarragon sauce
1 cup fresh tarragon leaves
3 cloves garlic, peeled and crushed
¼ cup white wine vinegar
½ cup olive oil
1 Tbsp castor sugar
salt to taste
black pepper to taste
1 cup crème fraîche (or more to taste)
1 Tbsp capers, rinsed

Preheat the oven to 180 °C.

Place the potatoes in a deep ovenproof dish and sprinkle over the oil and salt, as well as the crushed garlic cloves and rosemary. If using, add the whole bulb of garlic to the dish as well.

Roast the potatoes for 50–60 minutes, shaking the dish occasionally, until they are golden-brown and their skins are crispy. Serve warm with lamb neck, pan juices and the tarragon sauce.

For the tarragon sauce
Place the tarragon, garlic, vinegar, oil, sugar, salt and pepper in a blender and blitz. Transfer to a bowl, stir in the crème fraîche and capers and set aside until ready to serve.

TIP: You can also dry canned chickpeas with paper towel and deep fry them, to serve over the tarragon sauce.

Since I first ate these in Sweden, I refuse to prepare potatoes any other way.

Vegetable sosaties

1 sweet red pepper, pith
   removed and cut into
   2-cm cubes
2 red onions, peeled and cut
   into 2-cm cubes
3 courgettes, sliced on
   the diagonal
12 whole button mushrooms
6 patty pans, halved
6 wooden skewers, soaked in
   water for 20 minutes
2 Tbsp olive oil
a pinch of salt
pepper to taste

Sweet chilli sauce
½ cup light soy sauce
1 Tbsp sweet chilli sauce
a little sesame seed oil
   to taste
a little white wine vinegar
   to taste

Alternately thread pieces of red pepper, onion, courgette, mushrooms and patty pans onto the skewers. Brush with olive oil and season with salt and pepper. Braai over medium coals until lightly browned and soft.

Combine the sauce ingredients and serve with the sosaties.

TIP: You could add cubes of cooked chicken, beef or pork, and serve the sosaties on fried noodles.

Prepared over a braai, these sosaties
look beautiful on a tapas platter.

Comfort food

The food my grandmother Katy from Sutherland made always comforted me. It's my hope that *Taste the Little Karoo* will inspire you to prepare dishes to comfort your loved ones by using locally available ingredients. Not everything needs a 'twist'. I love making traditional Little Karoo favourites such as *vetkoek*, *melkkos* and rich soups, and just serving them differently, with unusual accompaniments.

My *melkkos*

Serves 6

1½ cups cake flour, sifted
½ tsp salt
40 g cold butter, cut into small cubes
4 cups milk
1 piece stick cinnamon
1 bay leaf
1 star anise
½ cup cold milk
cinnamon-sugar for serving

Combine the flour and salt. Using your fingertips, rub the butter into the flour until the mixture resembles fine breadcrumbs.

In a saucepan, heat the milk, cinnamon, bay leaf and star anise, then bring to the boil. Reduce the heat, then remove the cinnamon, bay leaf and star anise.

Mix a little of the flour mixture with the cold milk until well combined, then blend it into the hot milk using a stick blender. Continue to blend while gradually adding the rest of the flour mixture to the hot milk. (A stick blender will produce a silky-soft mixture.) Simmer for 8–10 minutes, stirring continuously. Remove from the heat and spoon into warm bowls.

Serve hot, generously sprinkled with cinnamon-sugar.

When I was a child, this dish, which is like a thick white sauce, was my soul food. A bowl of hot 'melkkos' with lots of cinnamon-sugar, enjoyed in front of the fire on a Sunday evening, is something every child should experience.

Barley soup

Serves 8

¼ cup canola oil
500 g stewing mutton, cubed
1 onion, peeled and
   finely chopped
2 tsp coarse salt
2 carrots, grated
2 turnips, grated
¼ cup finely chopped
   sweet green pepper
250 g pearl barley, soaked
   in water
4 medium potatoes, peeled
   and chopped
8 cups boiling water
8 cups beef stock
½ cup finely chopped
   fresh soup celery
freshly ground black pepper
   to taste
white pepper to taste
½ cup finely chopped
   fresh parsley

Heat the oil in a deep saucepan and brown the meat with the onion and salt. Add the carrots, turnips and green pepper and fry. Add the barley and potatoes, then cover with boiling water and stock. Simmer for a few minutes, then add the celery. Gradually add more water as the soup thickens. Cook until the meat and barley are tender.

About 10 minutes before serving, season with black and white pepper and sprinkle in the parsley.

My mom always offered us barley soup as we entered the house, and I still remember its clean and simple taste, as well as how good it was for me.

Serves 6–8

olive oil for frying

4 onions, peeled and sliced

4 cloves garlic, peeled
and crushed

2 tsp coarse salt

500 g beef chunks and
a few marrowbones

2 tsp hot curry powder

2 tsp paprika

6 tomatoes, plunged into
boiling water and skinned

¼ cup tomato purée

2 x 410-g cans tomato-and-
onion mix

2 cups sliced brown mushrooms

2 Tbsp wild mushroom
powder or powdered stock
(see page 23)

410-g can butter beans,
drained

2 cups dried speckled beans,
soaked in water overnight,
then drained and rinsed

410-g can kidney beans,
drained

410-g can baked beans in
tomato sauce

1 cup lentils, soaked in water
for 1 hour, then drained
and rinsed

6–8 cups beef stock

salt and freshly ground black
pepper to taste

2 each red and green chillies,
seeded and finely chopped
(optional) (keep the seeds
if you like extra-spicy food)

finely chopped fresh parsley
for garnishing

Four-bean tomato soup with beef and mushrooms

In a large saucepan, heat the oil and fry the onions, garlic and salt until the onions are translucent. Add the beef and marrowbones and stir well. Add the curry powder and paprika, followed by the tomatoes, tomato purée and tomato-and-onion mix, and stir well before the curry powder and paprika start to burn. Add the mushrooms, mushroom powder or powdered stock, all the beans, lentils and stock. Simmer over medium heat for about 3 hours, stirring regularly.

Season with salt and pepper, then sprinkle over the chopped chillies (if using) and chopped parsley. Serve warm.

I use lots of chillies in this dish. Sometimes I freeze the soup so that I can serve it in a hurry, with freshly baked molasses bread (see page 56) and cheese, if guests arrive unexpectedly. It's also on my Alfresco Deli winter menu.

Serves 6–8

1 Tbsp butter
canola oil, to taste
500 g firm-fleshed white fish,
  cut into chunks
1 cup shelled mussels
1 cup shelled shrimps
1 cup crayfish chunks (or
  more if preferred)
6–8 porcini, white or brown
  mushrooms, sliced
½ sweet yellow pepper,
  finely chopped
1 Tbsp finely chopped
  fresh thyme
1 tsp grated fresh ginger
  (optional)
½ tsp chilli flakes (optional)
1 Tbsp fish spice
½ cup chardonnay
5 spring onions, finely
  chopped
1 Tbsp finely chopped fresh dill
1 tsp saffron powder or
  5 threads saffron
1 tsp paprika
1 tsp ground turmeric
a pinch of ground coriander
  (optional)
410-g can coconut milk
¼ cup freshly squeezed
  lime juice
2 Tbsp fish sauce or to taste
1 tsp Maldon salt or to taste
1 cup sour cream (optional)
freshly ground black and red
  pepper mixture to taste
chopped fresh coriander
  for garnishing

Stock

fish bones, celery, carrots,
  onions, lemon juice and
  fish spice to taste
1 cup dry white wine
16 cups water

Meyer's fish soup with spring onions and crayfish

First prepare the stock by placing all the ingredients into a large saucepan, then simmering until reduced to 12 cups. Strain through a sieve, discard the bones and return the liquid to the saucepan. Set aside until needed.

Heat the butter and oil in a large pan and quickly seal the fish and seafood. Set aside. Fry the mushrooms and yellow pepper in the same pan, then add the thyme, ginger and chilli (if using), and fish spice.

Transfer the mushroom mixture to the large saucepan containing the stock and add the chardonnay, spring onions and dill. Mix the saffron, paprika, turmeric and ground coriander (if using) with a little coconut milk, then add this paste and the remaining coconut milk, lime juice and fish sauce to the stock. Simmer until the soup has thickened and reduced to your liking. Add the fish and seafood and simmer gently for 10 minutes or until just cooked. If using sour cream, add it now to thicken the soup further. (I prefer this soup with a somewhat runny consistency.) Season generously with black and red pepper and garnish with the fresh coriander just before serving.

Believe me, we do eat fish and seafood in the Little Karoo — after all, we need the good omegas too. I serve this soup with freshly baked olive ciabatta (see page 55).

Nita's quirky *roosterkoek* and *vetkoek*

Makes 20 *roosterkoek* or 25 small *vetkoek*

4 cups cake flour, sifted
10-g sachet instant dry yeast
1 tsp salt
1 tsp sugar
lukewarm water
canola oil for deep-frying
   the *vetkoek*

Vetkoek filling
¼ cup biltong shavings mixed
   with a ¼ cup *moskonfyt*
   (must preserve) or
   grape jam
OR
¼ cup dukkah mixed with
   ¼ cup tomato and
   chilli jam

To prepare the dough for either the *roosterkoek* (griddle cakes) or the *vetkoek* (fat cakes), mix the flour, yeast, salt and sugar together with enough lukewarm water to form a stiff dough. Knead the dough on a floured surface until smooth and elastic. Place in a greased bowl and leave to rise, covered with a thick cloth, for about 2 hours, until doubled in size.

For the *roosterkoek*
On a lightly floured surface, roll out the dough to about 2 cm thick and leave to rise to about 5 cm thick. Cut into squares and place on a floured baking tray. Braai on a grid over medium coals, turning the grid regularly. Serve with butter, apricot jam and boerewors.

For the *vetkoek*
When the dough is ready, knock it down a bit, then pinch off bits and shape them into balls. Using your thumb, make a hollow in each ball and place a teaspoonful of your chosen filling into it (ensure that the filling isn't too runny). Pinch the sides of the dough to seal in the filling. Don't over work the dough and make sure that there is no filling on your hands, which can smear onto the outside of the dough balls.

   Pour the oil to halfway in a deep saucepan and heat until piping hot. Using a slotted spoon, carefully lower the dough balls into the hot oil. Deep-fry until the balls are golden-brown. Usually the balls will turn over when one side is done. Remove and drain on a wire rack.

TIP: I give *roosterkoek* a Mediterranean twist by placing a teaspoonful of hummus and balsamic onion marmalade on top and serving them with oven-roasted vegetables such as butternut and brinjal, or feta and finely sliced biltong, either way rounded off with fresh herbs, or with *moskonfyt* and shavings of any strong Dutch cheese.

These are some of the most traditional — and often underrated — foods of the Little Karoo, but what could be more delicious than a 'vetkoek' or 'roosterkoek'?

Sheet music bread

Makes ± 12 rounds

10-g sachet instant dry yeast
5 cups cake flour, sifted
2 cups lukewarm water
3 Tbsp butter, melted,
   for sweet bread or 3 Tbsp
   olive oil for savoury bread
   (e.g. pita)
1 Tbsp sugar
2 tsp salt
butter or non-stick
   cooking spray
poppy seeds for sprinkling

Mix the yeast and 3 cups of the cake flour in a mixing bowl. Add the water, melted butter or olive oil, sugar and salt, then mix well. Gradually add more flour until the dough becomes pliable; if it is too firm it will be difficult to work with and the end product will be dry.

On a lightly floured surface, knead the dough for about 3 minutes until smooth and elastic. Sprinkle lightly with flour and shape into a neat ball. Return the dough to the bowl, cover and leave to rise for 30–40 minutes, until doubled in size.

Preheat the oven to 200 °C and grease 2 large baking trays with butter or non-stick cooking spray.

Knock down the risen dough and divide it into 4 portions, then divide each portion into 3 balls. Place the balls on a floured surface, cover and leave to rest for 15 minutes to relax the dough.

Roll out each dough ball as thinly as possible to make a circle of 10–12 cm in diameter. Sprinkle the dough lightly with poppy seeds and lightly press the seeds into the dough. (If you prefer flatbreads, prick the dough before baking to prevent the bread from puffing up.) Arrange the circles on the prepared baking trays and bake for about 8 minutes, until puffy, crisp and light golden-brown. Leave to cool on a wire rack.

These thin, crispy bread rounds originated in Sardinia. They are particularly delicious with flavoured cream cheese, biltong or brinjal pâté, liver spread and tapenade. This recipe was inspired by Carolie de Koster.

Focaccia

3½ cups bread flour, plus
　extra for sifting

1 cup fine semolina

2 tsp coarse sea salt

10-g sachet instant dry yeast

½ tsp sugar

1 cup lukewarm water

canola oil

olive oil to taste

Balsamic onion topping

2 Tbsp olive oil

2 shallots or onions, peeled
　and chopped

2 spring onions, chopped

2 red onions, peeled and
　finely sliced

a few sprigs of fresh thyme,
　leaves removed

coarse salt to taste

¼ cup balsamic vinegar

Basil pesto, cherry tomato and cheese topping

¼ cup basil pesto

10 ripe cherry tomatoes

coarse salt and freshly ground
　black pepper to taste

olive oil to taste

2–3 Tbsp white grape vinegar

2 cloves garlic, peeled
　and sliced

6 anchovy fillets, chopped

2 tsp pine nuts, toasted

2 feta rounds, crumbled,
　plus 3 Tbsp blue cheese or
　goat's milk cheese

OR

1 cup grated pecorino or
　Gruyère, plus ½ cup
　grated Parmesan

a sprig of fresh rosemary,
　leaves removed

Place the flour, semolina and salt in a large mixing bowl. In a separate bowl, mix together the yeast, sugar and water. Make a well in the flour mixture and slowly pour in the yeast mixture. When it starts to froth, stir with a fork until well combined. Knead the dough vigorously for about 5 minutes until smooth, elastic and soft.

Grease a large bowl lightly with oil and transfer the dough to the bowl. Sift over a little extra flour, cover with a thick cloth and leave to rise for about 30 minutes, until doubled in size.

Preheat the oven to 220 °C. Grease a baking tray with canola oil.

When the dough has risen, place it on the prepared baking tray and spread it out to the desired shape. Using your fingertips, press into the dough to make several indentations. Drizzle over some olive oil and add the toppings (as described below).

For the balsamic onion topping (first layer)

In a pan, heat the olive oil and fry the shallots or onions, spring onions, red onions, thyme leaves and salt until the onions are soft. Add the balsamic vinegar and cook for a few minutes until the mixture has thickened. Leave to cool before spreading over the focaccia dough.

For the basil pesto, cherry tomato and cheese topping (second layer)

Place the basil pesto and cherry tomatoes in a bowl. Season with the salt, pepper, olive oil and vinegar. Mix in the garlic and anchovy fillets, then spread over the first layer. Sprinkle the pine nuts on top followed by the cheese mixture of your choice. Finally, scatter over the rosemary leaves and drizzle with some olive oil. Leave to rise for 10 minutes, then bake for 20 minutes until golden-brown.

TIP: You can use more anchovy fillets in the second layer if you prefer a stronger fish flavour.

You can serve this focaccia as a starter.

Tradouw ciabattas with dried figs or olives

Makes 2 medium ciabattas

4½ cups cake flour, sifted
¼ sachet (2.5 g) instant
   dry yeast
¾ tsp coarse salt
¼ tsp sugar
2½ cups lukewarm water
sunflower oil for greasing
¼ cup chopped dried figs
¼ cup olives, pitted
   and chopped
olive oil for drizzling
   (optional)

In a the bowl of an electric mixer and using a dough hook, mix the flour, yeast, salt, sugar and water until it forms a soft dough that isn't too runny. If it is too runny, add a little more flour; if it is too dry, add a little extra lukewarm water. Knead for 5–10 minutes.

Grease a large bowl with sunflower oil, then place the dough in the bowl and leave to rise for about 1 hour, until doubled in size and bubbles form in the dough.

Preheat the oven to 250 °C and lightly grease a baking tray with sunflower oil.

Tip the dough onto a well-floured surface and, working gently, divide it in half. Knead the figs into one half and the olives into the other. Using your hands, shape the dough into ciabatta ovals and place them on the prepared baking tray. Make flour 'paths' between the ciabattas to prevent them from running into one another. Bake for 10–15 minutes. As soon as the crusts start to form, reduce the heat to 180 °C and bake for a further 25–30 minutes, until the crusts have browned. Remove from the oven, drizzle with olive oil (if using) and serve hot.

The Italian word 'ciabatta' means 'slipper', describing the bread's oval, slipper-like shape.

The best molasses bread

Makes 4 loaves

⅓ cup molasses
2 Tbsp brown sugar
¼ cup honey
4 cups lukewarm water
2.5-kg pack brown bread
  flour, sifted
10-g sachet instant dry yeast
1 Tbsp salt
seeds of your choice (sesame,
  sunflower, poppy and/
  or pumpkin seeds) for
  sprinkling

Preheat the oven to 180 °C. Grease four 15 x 28-cm loaf tins.

In a bowl, mix together the molasses, sugar, honey and water until combined. In another bowl, mix the flour, yeast and salt together, then gradually stir into the molasses mixture until it forms a smooth dough. Spoon the dough into the prepared loaf tins, filling each to halfway. Leave to rise in the tins until three-quarters full.

Sprinkle the seeds in rows over the loaves and bake for about 1 hour, until the sides loosen. Remove from the oven and leave to cool slightly in the tins before turning out the loaves.

Serve warm with farm butter.

At the deli we bake this bread almost every day — it's really delicious served with liver pâté, onion marmalade, toasted sesame seeds and fresh parsley.

Blini with spring onion

Makes ± 18

1½ cups cake flour, sifted
1½ cups self-raising
   flour, sifted
1 cup bran
1 tsp salt
10-g sachet instant dry yeast
2 tsp sugar
½ cup lukewarm water
1 cup milk
3 eggs, separated
3 Tbsp butter, melted
chopped spring onions
canola oil for frying

In a mixing bowl, mix together the flours, bran and salt. In a separate bowl, mix the yeast, sugar and water together until the sugar and yeast have dissolved. Stir in the milk, egg yolks and butter. Make a well in the flour mixture and pour the milk mixture into it, followed by the spring onions. Mix until the batter is smooth, then cover with a thick cloth and set aside in a warm place for about 1 hour, until doubled in volume. Beat the egg whites until stiff and fold into the batter.

Heat some oil in a deep frying pan and drop spoonfuls of the batter into the oil. Leave enough room for spreading. Fry until golden-brown and bubbles form on the surface. Flip over and fry until done. Drain on paper towel.

TIP: Serve blini with steamed fresh asparagus, crème fraîche or creamed cottage cheese with deep-fried capers and freshly ground black pepper, or with smoked salmon and dill.

Makes ± 16

canola oil for deep-frying

Pastry
3 cups cake flour, sifted
1 tsp salt
¼ cup sunflower oil
1 egg yolk, beaten
± 1 cup water

Filling
2 Tbsp sunflower oil for frying
1 onion, peeled and finely
    chopped
2 cloves garlic, crushed
1 tsp coarse salt
500 g mince (a mixture of
    lamb and beef)
a splash of white wine
1 tsp braai spice
1 tsp curry powder
1 tsp chilli powder
1 tsp mustard powder
1 tsp turmeric
½ tsp toasted cumin seeds
1 red chilli, finely chopped
½ tsp grated fresh ginger
freshly ground black pepper
    to taste
1 tsp chopped fresh mint
1 tsp chopped fresh coriander
juice of ½ lemon

Little Karoo samoosas

For the pastry
Combine the flour and salt in a mixing bowl. Make a well in the flour mixture and pour in the oil, egg yolk and enough water to form a stiff dough. Knead on a floured surface until smooth, then shape the dough into a ball. Cover with clingfilm and refrigerate for 30 minutes.

For the filling
Heat the oil in a frying pan, add the onion, garlic and salt, then fry until soft and golden-brown. Add the mince and wine and fry until the mince is cooked. Stir in all the spices and fry until all the ingredients are well combined. Remove from the heat and stir through the fresh mint and coriander, as well as the lemon juice. Set aside to cool.

For the samoosas
Divide the pastry into 8 equal pieces. Roll each piece into a ball. On a floured surface, roll out the balls to a thickness of 3–4 mm and measuring 15–20 cm in diameter. Cut each circle in half using a knife. With the straight side of a semi-circle facing left, brush the straight side with a little water. Fold the bottom corner towards the centre of the right curved edge. Then fold the flap up to meet the top corner to form a cone shape. Place a heaped tablespoon of filling inside each cone. Brush a little more water on the inside edges and press together to seal. Repeat until all the semi-circles have been filled.

Half-fill a deep saucepan with oil and heat until warm. Deep-fry the samoosas for 3–5 minutes until golden-brown. Drain on paper towels.

Serves 6–8

3 Tbsp butter, melted
coarse salt to taste
1 tsp cayenne pepper
1 tsp white pepper
freshly squeezed lemon juice
   to taste
4 x 250-g kudu fillets
6–8 pita breads (see page 186)

Salsa

8 small ripe tomatoes, halved
1 large red onion, peeled
   and chopped
a handful of fresh basil, torn
a handful baby spinach, torn
1 red chilli, finely chopped
¼ cup balsamic reduction
coarse salt and freshly ground
   black pepper to taste

Mayonnaise

¼ cup olive oil
2 tsp prepared Dijon mustard
¼ cup mayonnaise
2 egg yolks
coarse salt and freshly ground
   black pepper to taste
1 clove garlic, crushed

Pita bread with kudu fillet, salsa and mustard mayonnaise

Mix together the ingredients for the salsa in one bowl, then do the same for the mayonnaise in another bowl. Set both aside until ready to serve.

Mix the melted butter, salt, peppers and lemon juice together and rub over the fillets. Heat a griddle pan and fry each fillet for 5 minutes on each side – the meat should be tender and pink on the inside. Remove from the pan and leave to rest for about 5 minutes before cutting into pieces. Spoon some fillet, salsa and mayonnaise into each pita and serve warm.

TIP: These pitas are also delicious served with chicken strips. Replace the salsa with tzatziki or thinly sliced cucumber. Add vegetables such as butternut and brinjal, then top with onion marmalade, feta and fresh herbs.

Hot cross buns

Makes 12

3½ cups cake flour, sifted
2 Tbsp softened butter
10-g sachet instant dry yeast
1 Tbsp white sugar
1 tsp salt
1 tsp ground cinnamon
1 tsp mixed spice
½ tsp ground nutmeg
1 egg, beaten
1 cup lukewarm milk
50 g pecan nuts, chopped
50 g seedless raisins

Crosses
½ cup cake flour, sifted
½ cup water
1 egg yolk, beaten

To make the buns, place the flour in a bowl then rub in the butter, using your fingertips. Add the yeast, sugar, salt, cinnamon, mixed spice and nutmeg and mix well. Stir in the egg and milk to form a soft, pliable dough. Knead well for about 5 minutes. Add the nuts and raisins and knead for at least another 10 minutes. Place the dough in a large greased bowl and cover with clingfilm. Leave to rise in a warm place until doubled in size.

Preheat the oven to 180 °C. Grease or spray a 28 x 18-cm baking tray.

Knock down the dough and shape it into 12 buns. Pack the buns closely together in the prepared tin and cover with a kitchen cloth. Leave to rise in a warm place.

In the meanwhile, prepare the mixture for the crosses. Mix the flour and water to form a smooth paste. Make a piping bag from baking paper and fill with the paste.

Brush the buns with the beaten egg yolk. Pipe a cross onto each bun. Bake for 30–35 minutes, then serve warm.

Children will enjoy helping you to make these buns. Serve them with cheeses on a cheese board as a starter, or with pickled fish for Easter. In winter, they taste heavenly with strong cheese, grape jam and a cup of coffee.

Unleavened flatbread

Makes 3 flatbreads

1½ cups white bread flour
1 tsp salt
1 Tbsp olive oil
½ cup lukewarm water
your choice of toppings (see
    Topping suggestions)

Sift the flour and salt together in a bowl. In another bowl, mix together the olive oil and water. Gradually stir the oil-and-water mixture into the flour mixture until it forms a pliable dough (the amount of water may vary from time to time). Place the dough on a floured surface and knead until smooth and elastic. Cover with a moist cloth or clingfilm and leave to rest for about 20 minutes.

Divide the dough into three equal pieces, shape into balls and roll out into thin circles, or rectangles, which I usually serve as pizza portions.

Heat a non-stick electric frying pan or griddle pan and fry the circles or rectangles until they start to blister and brown. Turn them over and fry the other side until golden-brown. Remove from the pan and serve hot with a topping of your choice (see below).

Topping suggestions

- Jersey beef fillet strips marinated in red wine, olive oil and lemon juice, then flash-fried with coarse salt. When cool, mix with tzatziki and mint leaves.
- Mix crème fraîche and capers and serve atop salmon or pickled fish. Drizzle with a teaspoon of balsamic vinegar and sprinkle over fresh herbs.
- Serve the flatbreads with ostrich carpaccio, melted brie cheese, berry jus and rocket leaves.
- Children enjoy them with mozzarella, coppa ham, homemade tomato *smoor* and olive tapenade.

This recipe, courtesy of www.pasella.com, is so tasty and so easy. I sometimes use it to make small pizzas for a quick meal.

Fresh

An innovative salad with tasty bread is a meal in itself. But salads can also be simple, needing nothing more than a delicious dressing or infused olive oil, and served as a starter or side dish. Here in the Little Karoo we believe that salads are a way to enjoy fruit and vegetables straight from the earth, fresh and pure. Our own kitchen garden provides us with brinjals, butternuts, beetroot and lettuce. Enjoy these nutritious salads and dressings.

Serves 6–8

± 600 g butter lettuce leaves
1 cup Jersey beef (or any
   moist beef) biltong strips
1 cup dry venison
   biltong strips
½ cup chopped blue cheese
½ cup crumbled feta
1 avocado, cut into strips
2 oranges, peeled and thinly
   sliced
2 naartjies, segmented
12 slices Granny Smith apples
12 slices Pink Lady apples
3 Tbsp pomegranate arils
6–8 baby beetroots, boiled
   and halved
± 15 radicchio leaves, torn
12 green olives, pitted
12 black olives, pitted
½ cup gooseberries
¼ cup sunflower
   seeds, toasted
salted mixed nuts,
   lightly toasted

Dressing
¾ cup avocado oil
2 Tbsp balsamic vinegar
1 tsp chopped garlic
2 tsp brown sugar
1 tsp honey
3 Tbsp freshly sqeezed
   orange juice

Tradouw Jersey biltong salad

Mix the dressing ingredients together until well combined. Arrange all the salad ingredients in a bowl or on a serving dish, as preferred. Pour the dressing over the salad.

As an alternative to the moist Jersey biltong and dry venison biltong, I sometimes use ostrich fillets cut into strips, marinated in red wine, balsamic vinegar and dukkah, then flash-fried in a griddle pan.

Serves 6

1 medium pack fresh mixed
   herb greens
1 small head butter lettuce,
   shredded
15 black olives, pitted
10 strawberries, hulled and
   halved
20 fine baby green beans,
   lightly steamed
½ x 410-g can whole
   baby corn
20 thin Gruyère shavings
1 Tbsp olive caviar (optional)
10 thin slices coppa or Parma
   ham or prosciutto (optional)
a few strips of oven-roasted
   sweet green pepper
   (optional)
a handful of almonds, toasted
2 Tbsp sunflower
   seeds, toasted
2 Tbsp sesame seeds,
   toasted (optional)
balsamic reduction (optional)

Tradouw dressing
1 tsp prepared Dijon mustard
½ cup olive oil
2 Tbsp freshly squeezed lemon
   juice (or more to taste)
1 tsp coarse salt
freshly ground black pepper
   to taste
1 tsp white sugar
1 Tbsp white wine vinegar
1 tsp mayonnaise or cream
   (optional)

Gruyère salad

Mix the dressing ingredients together using a hand mixer, or shake them well in a jar. Arrange the salad ingredients, except the almonds, seeds and balsamic reduction, on a large serving platter or in a bowl. Pour the dressing over the salad and sprinkle over the almonds and seeds, then drizzle over the balsamic reduction, if using.

This classic salad is a popular choice on the deli menu.

Beate's Caesar salad

Serves 8

1 sweet red pepper
1 medium-large pack cos
  lettuce leaves (preferably
  small, young leaves)
5 eggs (preferably free
  range), medium or hard-
  boiled and halved
½ cup crumbled blue cheese
a handful of fresh herbs (e.g.
  rocket), finely chopped
1 onion, thinly sliced
1 Tbsp sunflower
  seeds, toasted
1 Tbsp pumpkin
  seeds, toasted
a few anchovy fillets, halved
15 capers, deep fried for
  garnishing
1 tsp Maldon salt
freshly ground black pepper
  to taste
balsamic reduction to taste

Croutons
4 tsp olive oil
crushed garlic to taste
coarse salt to taste
2 slices ciabatta

Dressing
± 10 anchovy fillets (with oil)
¼ cup olive oil
2 Tbsp freshly squeezed
  lemon juice
3 egg yolks
2 cloves garlic, peeled
  and crushed
2 Tbsp mayonnaise
2 Tbsp cream or thick yoghurt
a pinch of Maldon salt
  (optional)

To make the croutons, combine the olive oil, garlic and salt. Cut the ciabatta into 16 cubes or chunks, then add them to the olive oil mixture and shake to coat. Heat a pan over medium heat and fry the ciabatta pieces until golden-brown, taking care not to burn the bread. Set the croutons aside until ready to use.

Using a hand-held blender, mix together all the dressing ingredients (including the oil from the anchovy fillets) until smooth and well combined.

Grill the red pepper under the grill of an oven until scorched and blackened. Immediately place it in a plastic bag to sweat until it is tender and wrinkled. Remove the skin and cut the flesh into thin strips.

Pile the cos lettuce onto a serving plate or in a bowl, then pour over the dressing. Arrange the eggs and croutons on top, followed by the blue cheese, herbs and onion.

Sprinkle all the seeds over the salad and arrange the red pepper strips and anchovies on top. Finally, sprinkle over the capers, season with salt and pepper and a drizzle of balsamic reduction, if using.

I had the best Caesar salad ever in California, and since then it has been my favourite salad. The secret is to make your own dressing and to make sure the croutons are not too oily.

Serves 8

¼ cup dukkah (see page 189)
12 thin slices butternut
¼ cup grated Parmesan
12 thin slices brinjal
1 medium pack rocket leaves
6 cooked whole beetroots
    (baby and large), halved
    (or beetroots pickled in
    ginger sold by farm delis)
4 rounds feta, roughly
    crumbled
fresh herbs for garnishing
2 tsp sesame seeds, toasted
a few slices mozzarella
⅓ cup hummus (see page 189)
balsamic reduction
freshly ground black pepper
    to taste

Basil vinaigrette foam (optional)

2 tsp gelatine powder
¼ cup warm water
3 Tbsp freshly squeezed
    lemon juice
¼ cup olive oil
1 tsp white wine vinegar
1 cup roughly chopped
    fresh basil leaves
½ tsp cayenne pepper
3 egg whites, beaten with a
    pinch of cream of tartar
    until stiff
salt and pepper to taste

Beate's vegetable salad

Preheat the oven to 200 °C.

Sprinkle the dukkah over the butternut and the Parmesan over the brinjal. Place the butternut and brinjal in a greased ovenproof dish and roast in the oven until crisp. Remove and leave to cool.

Arrange the rocket leaves on a serving platter, then pile the cooled butternut and brinjal on top, followed by the beetroot and half of the feta. Garnish with the fresh herbs, sesame seeds, remaining feta and mozzarella. Dot the hummus on the outer edges of the platter. (You could even add Chickpea and spring onion balls (see page 16) to the salad.) If you like, sprinkle over more dukkah and Parmesan. Drizzle balsamic reduction over and season with salt and pepper.

To make the vinaigrette, dissolve the gelatine in the water. Mix together the dissolved gelatine, lemon juice, olive oil, vinegar, basil and cayenne pepper well combined. Refrigate until cool. Stir through the whisked egg whites just before serving and season with salt and pepper.

Drizzle the vinaigrette over the salad. It will not keep its foamy consistency for long, so use it immediately once made.

This unusual vegetable salad creates that 'wow' factor on any table!

Serves 20

1 whole green cabbage,
  finely chopped
1 medium red cabbage,
  finely chopped
500 g carrots, peeled and
  finely grated
3 x 73-g packets 2-minute
  noodles, broken up
½ cup sesame seeds, toasted
½ cup sunflower
  seeds, toasted
½ cup pumpkin
  seeds, toasted
½ cup dried cranberries
½ cup dukkah
2 cups shredded fresh
  coriander for garnishing

Dressing

1 cup dark brown sugar
2 cups balsamic vinegar or
  red wine vinegar
1 cup soy sauce
½ cup honey
2 Tbsp freshly squeezed
  lemon juice
2 tsp wholegrain mustard
1 tsp prepared English
  mustard or mustard
  powder
½ tsp freshly ground black
  pepper
½ tsp white pepper

Cabbage and carrot salad

Place all the dressing ingredients in a small saucepan over medium heat and bring to the boil. Stir until reduced by a quarter, then remove from the heat and set aside to cool.

In a round, deep glass bowl, arrange the green and red cabbage and carrots in layers on top of one another; be careful not to mix the layers. Sprinkle over the noodles, followed by the seeds, cranberries and dukkah. Drizzle over the dressing, then garnish with the coriander.

Indonesian in origin, this salad is perfect for serving to large groups of people.

Serves 6–8

400 g butter lettuce leaves
1 cup fresh herb leaves,
    e.g. rocket or coriander
1 cup chopped baby spinach
1 cup chopped baby
    watercress
12 dried figs, chopped and
    soaked in port
4 ripe soft-eating white pears,
    sliced lengthwise
125 g blue cheese (or more),
    crumbled
½ cup chopped walnuts
10 slices Parma ham or
    prosciutto (optional)
1 Tbsp sunflower
    seeds, toasted
1 Tbsp sesame seeds, toasted,
    for garnishing
1 Tbsp pine nuts, toasted
2 Tbsp finely chopped
    fresh mint
balsamic reduction
coarse salt and freshly
ground black pepper

Vinaigrette
¾ cup pomegranate juice
½ cup castor sugar
2 Tbsp (or more) dried
    cranberries
2 tsp gelatine powder
¼ cup olive oil
2 Tbsp plain yoghurt (optional)
torn fresh mint to taste

Pear, blue cheese and walnut salad

To make the vinaigrette, place the pomegranate juice, sugar and cranberries in a small saucepan over high heat and bring to the boil, stirring until the sugar has dissolved. Mix the gelatine powder with a little of the warm sauce until dissolved, then whisk into the sauce. Refrigerate until thickened, then stir in the olive oil, yoghurt and mint.

Arrange the butter lettuce leaves on a platter, then scatter over the herbs, spinach, watercress, figs, pears, blue cheese, walnuts, ham (if using), seeds, nuts and chopped mint. Drizzle over the vinaigrette and balsamic reduction, then season with salt and pepper.

This remains one of my favourite flavour combinations.

Serves 8

½ cup freshly squeezed
    lemon juice
2 Tbsp soy sauce
1 Tbsp sesame seeds, toasted
1 tsp Maldon salt
500 g tuna steak
¼ cup olive oil
½ cup coarsely grated
    Parmesan cheese
1 medium head butter lettuce
6 soft-boiled quails' eggs or
    small free-range eggs
1 cup black olives, pitted
2 cups cherry tomatoes,
    quartered
350 g fine green beans,
    blanched and immediately
    plunged into iced water
½ red onion, peeled and
    finely sliced into rings
thin slices of lemon
    for garnishing
Parmesan shavings
    for garnishing
a handful of capers
    for garnishing
1 cup fresh rocket
    for garnishing
freshly ground black pepper

Herb dressing

½ cup olive oil
¼ cup water
1 tsp finely chopped garlic
1 Tbsp white wine vinegar
8 anchovy fillets with oil,
    chopped
a large handful of fresh
    basil, chopped
grated zest of 1 lemon
1 onion, peeled and finely
    sliced into rings
4 courgettes, topped, tailed
    and thinly sliced
8 Peppadews, chopped

My niçoise salad

For the herb dressing, blend the olive oil, water, garlic, vinegar, anchovy fillets and their oil, basil and lemon zest in a blender until well combined. Add the onion, courgettes and Peppadews, then set aside until ready to use..

Mix the lemon juice, soy sauce and sesame seeds in a small bowl. Sprinkle the salt over the tuna. Heat the olive oil in a griddle pan and fry the tuna for about 2 minutes while drizzling the lemon juice mixture over it. Remove from the pan and set aside to cool.

Sprinkle the grated Parmesan on a baking tray lined with baking paper and grill in the oven until the cheese is golden. Set aside to cool.

Arrange the butter lettuce leaves on a platter and scatter the grilled Parmesan over. Slice the tuna into thin strips and arrange on top of the leaves, followed by the eggs, olives, tomatoes, green beans and onion rings. Garnish with the lemon slices, Parmesan shavings, capers and rocket. Drizzle over the herb dressing, then season with pepper.

This very special, classic salad is a firm favourite.

Serves 6

3 fresh yellow freestone
peaches, halved or sliced

3 fresh nectarines, sliced

3 purple or yellow plums,
halved

3 ripe hard-eating
white pears, sliced

2 cups fresh figs, chopped

1 cup dried figs, halved and
soaked in port

10 cold prickly pears, peeled
and halved

10 each green and orange
melon balls (optional)

10 large strawberries, hulled
and halved

10 thin slices papaya

½ cup mixed salted nuts

2 Tbsp sunflower
seeds, toasted

2 Tbsp raw pumpkin
seeds, toasted

balsamic reduction for
garnishing

a few whole strawberries
for garnishing

2 sprigs fresh mint, finely
chopped for garnishing

Cranberry jus

1 cup dried cranberries

2 Tbsp brown sugar

2 Tbsp balsamic vinegar

¼ cup red wine

2 Tbsp port

¼ cup syrup from fig or
watermelon preserve

Mint apple slices

3 Tbsp castor sugar

seeds of 1 vanilla pod

1 stalk lemongrass, sliced

¼ cup fresh mint leaves,
chopped

3 sweet red apples, sliced

freshly squeezed lemon juice

Tradouw fruit salad

First make the cranberry jus by bringing all the jus ingredients to the boil in a saucepan over medium heat. Simmer until reduced by a quarter. Remove from the heat and allow to cool.

To prepare the mint apple slices, blend the sugar, vanilla seeds, lemongrass and mint until fine. Soak the apples in the lemon juice, then cover with the sugar mixture until all the apples are well coated.

Arrange the rest of the fruit on a serving dish or in a large bowl, followed by the apple slices. Sprinkle over the nuts and seeds. Drizzle the jus over everything, followed by the balsamic reduction. Garnish with the whole strawberries and mint.

TIP: Try to use readily available fresh fruit that is in season. If you're really stuck, you could substitute some canned alternatives, but not too many. There is always something in season – I use pineapple and apricots when peaches and pears are out of season.

This salad is exquisite if served with a fragrant bobotie or hot lamb curry.

Watermelon salad with gin and mint

Serves 10

⅔ cup gin
20 chunks crisp, cold
    watermelon
a handful of pumpkin
    seeds, toasted
a handful of sesame
    seeds, toasted
a handful of sunflower
    seeds, toasted
4 rounds black pepper feta,
    roughly crumbled
1 cup black olives, pitted
    and halved
a handful of capers,
    deep-fried
a spring of fresh mint for
    garnishing

Dressing
1 cup Bulgarian yoghurt
finely chopped fresh mint
    to taste

Sprinkle the gin over the watermelon chunks, then refrigerate.

In the meanwhile, make the dressing by mixing the yoghurt with the chopped mint.

Arrange the watermelon chunks on a flat plate and sprinkle over the pumpkin, sesame and sunflower seeds. Scatter the feta, olives and capers on top. Spoon the dressing lavishly over the salad and garnish with the mint leaves.

This salad tickles my imagination. My aunt Nolene always made it and I have been making my own version for years. Simply omit the alcohol if there are children among the diners. It's a firm favourite at Christmas — a refreshing al fresco dish that looks beautiful with its contrasting colours on a large plate.

1 garlic bulb, unpeeled

⅓ cup olive oil (more if necessary)

10 Mediterranean or waxy potatoes, boiled and halved (with skin)

15 whole new potatoes, boiled (with skin)

3 Tbsp butter

a few sprigs each of fresh thyme and rosemary

1 sweet red pepper, roasted, peeled and cut into strips

20 black olives

1 Tbsp sesame seeds, toasted

a handful of sunflower seeds, toasted

a handful of fresh flat-leaf parsley, shredded

freshly ground black pepper to taste

Onion marmalade

4 red onions, peeled and sliced into rings

3 Tbsp butter

1 Tbsp olive oil

½ cup balsamic vinegar

2 tsp brown sugar

15 capers

Mayonnaise dressing

2 Tbsp freshly squeezed lemon juice

3 egg yolks

3 Tbsp mayonnaise

1 Tbsp basil pesto

2 tsp prepared hot mustard

¼ cup olive oil

New potato salad with olives

To prepare the onion marmalade, cook the onions, butter, olive oil, vinegar and sugar together in a saucepan over medium heat until reduced to a thickish marmalade. Stir in the capers, cool and refrigerate until needed.

For the mayonnaise dressing, beat together the lemon juice, egg yolks, mayonnaise, pesto and mustard. Add the olive oil in a thin trickle, beating continuously until it becomes a thick sauce.

Preheat the oven to 180 °C.

Cut off the top of the garlic bulb, drizzle with olive oil and wrap in aluminium foil, then roast the garlic until browned and crisp (about 40 minutes). Once cool enough to handle, squeeze each clove in the bulb out of its skin.

Increase the oven temperature to 200 °C.

Place all the potatoes in a roasting dish, dot them with the butter, drizzle over some olive oil and scatter with the thyme and rosemary. Place a clove of garlic on each potato. Roast the potatoes until the skins are just beginning to crisp (about 30 minutes), shaking the tray often. Reduce the oven temperature to 150 °C and roast for an additional 30 minutes – until the potatoes' flesh is soft and the skins are even crunchier.

Arrange the potatoes on a serving plate and pour over some liquid from the roasting dish. Remove the herbs and leave the potatoes to cool. Spoon over the mayonnaise dressing, scatter the pepper strips and olives on top, then spoon over some onion marmalade. Sprinkle over the sesame and sunflower seeds, as well as the parsley and a grinding of black pepper.

Tempura baby asparagus

Serves 6

1 cup cornflour, sifted
2 egg whites, one runny, the
    other beaten until stiff
½ cup cold soda water
± 1 cup canola oil
300 g spears fresh baby
    asparagus
a pinch of paprika or cayenne
    pepper for garnishing

Using a hand mixer, mix together the cornflour, runny egg white and soda water until smooth and lump-free. Fold in the beaten egg white until it forms a light, lumpy batter.

Heat the oil in a deep frying pan. Dip 2 or 3 spears of asparagus at a time into the batter and deep-fry until lightly browned. Drain on paper towel. Serve with a sprinkling of paprika or cayenne pepper.

I usually serve these tempura asparagus over a sweetcorn salad (see page 82), and sometimes as a starter.

Serves 10

4 cups uncooked risoni (rice-
shaped pasta)
¼ cup basil pesto (see
page 189)
10 cherry tomatoes, halved
and fried in a griddle
pan with soy sauce and
olive oil
20 pitted green olives, whole
or halved
10 Peppadews, shredded
a handful of sunflower
seeds, toasted
a handful of pumpkin
seeds, toasted
a handful of salted
mixed nuts
1 cup canned chickpeas
4 wheels herbed feta,
roughly crumbled

Dressing

1 Tbsp freshly squeezed
lemon juice
2 Tbsp Greek yoghurt
(optional)
Tradouw salad dressing (see
page 67)

Carmen's Mediterranean risoni pasta salad

To make the dressing, mix the lemon juice and yoghurt (if using) with the Tradouw salad dressing.

Cook the risoni according to the packet instructions until tender. Stir the pesto through the pasta, then combine with the remaining ingredients, sprinkling some of the feta over the top. Serve the salad at room temperature, with the dressing alongside.

TIP: You can add any roasted or fried vegetables of your choice to this salad, such as cubed butternut and halved baby brinjals.

My sister once served this salad in the middle of the Little Karoo veld – it tasted better than ever.

Serves 8

4 mealies
coarse salt to taste
1 Tbsp butter
400 g butter lettuce leaves
1 red onion, peeled and finely
  chopped
10 each whole black and
  green olives, pitted
2 wheels feta, crumbled
1 avocado, flesh cubed
10 cherry tomatoes, halved
a handful of fresh coriander,
  finely chopped
wedges of lime
toasted nuts e.g. almonds, or
  sunflower seeds to taste
tempura baby asparagus
  (see page 79)
2 Tbsp cubed sweet red pepper

Chicken breasts

2 Tbsp olive oil
1 Tbsp sesame oil
1 Tbsp freshly squeezed
  lemon juice
1 Tbsp soy sauce
1 tsp paprika
1 tsp cayenne pepper
1 tsp sesame seeds, toasted
4 boneless chicken breasts,
  halved lengthwise
coarse salt and freshly ground
  black pepper to taste

Dressing

½ cup olive oil
½ cup coconut milk
1 tsp each finely chopped red
  and green chillies
2 Tbsp honey
finely grated zest and juice
  of 1 lime
1 cup cream-style sweetcorn
1 Tbsp finely chopped fresh
  coriander
1 clove garlic, finely chopped
1 tsp white sugar

Beate's sweetcorn salad

To prepare the chicken breasts, mix together the olive and sesame oils, lemon juice, soy sauce, paprika, cayenne pepper and seasame seeds, then rub thoroughly into the chicken breasts. Heat a griddle pan and fry the breasts for about 4 minutes on each side until cooked, but still pink inside (they will continue to cook while cooling). Season with salt and pepper, then leave to cool. Slice thinly and set aside until needed.

Use a hand mixer to make the dressing. Combine all the dressing ingredients and set aside.

In a saucepan of boiling salted water, cook the mealies until soft. Heat the butter in a griddle pan and fry the mealies until well browned, or grill over an open fire. Cut the corn off the cobs.

Arrange the butter lettuce leaves in a bowl or on a serving platter, followed by the the onion, olives, feta, avocado, tomatoes, fresh coriander, lime wedges, nuts and asparagus. Finally, add the chicken, corn, and red pepper on top. Drizzle over the dressing.

If you like, you could even serve this as a starter.

3 cups bulgur wheat
olive oil for frying
2 red onions, peeled and
    thinly sliced into rings
4 spring onions, finely
    chopped
1 sweet red pepper, pith
    removed and cubed
1 green chilli, deseeded
    and chopped
2 cloves garlic, peeled
    and crushed
½ cup canned chickpeas
    or to taste
2 tsp curry powder
½ tsp white pepper
¼ cup balsamic vinegar
1 cup chopped fresh celery
¼ cup chopped fresh parsley
1½ cups fresh or canned
    peach slices
¼ cup sunflower
    seeds, toasted
freshly ground black pepper
    to taste
fresh coriander for garnishing

Dressing

½ cup olive oil
2 Tbsp freshly squeezed
    lemon juice
1 tsp curry powder
½ tsp turmeric
1 Tbsp honey
1 tsp soy sauce
1 cup Bulgarian yoghurt

The Taljaards' wheat salad

For the dressing, mix together all the ingredients until well combined.

In a saucepan, pour in sufficient water to cover the wheat, then cook over medium heat until soft. Drain, rinse well and set aside to cool.

Heat the olive oil in a pan and fry all the onions, red pepper, chilli and garlic until the onions are soft. Add the chickpeas and curry powder and fry until the curry powder starts to cook. Remove from the heat and stir in the white pepper, vinegar, celery and parsley.

Mix the onion mixture, dressing and peach slices with the cooled wheat. Season with black pepper and garnish with the coriander. Serve at room temperature.

This versatile salad never disappoints and may be served with pork or a curry.

Gatherings

Nothing makes me happier than the spirit of sharing, and the Mediterranean way of preparing and serving food fuels my food inspiration. At Alfresco Deli we focus on platters, where every bite is a taste sensation, and good quality wine. Our Joubert-Tradauw vineyards and cellar borrow heavily from the European tradition of wine making, and wine and food pairing. I want people to think about what they're eating and to discover the bounty of the Little Karoo.

¼ cup sunflower oil

2 medium onions, peeled and finely chopped

2 cloves garlic, peeled and finely chopped

1 tsp coarse sea salt

1 Tbsp medium curry powder

1 Tbsp turmeric

1 tsp ground coriander

1 tsp ground cumin

1 tsp ground cinnamon

1.5 kg mixture of beef and ostrich mince

freshly squeezed juice of 2 lemons

1 Granny Smith apple, grated

2 tsp grated lemon zest

⅓ cup fruit chutney

1 cup fine white breadcrumbs

2 Tbsp soy sauce

freshly ground black pepper to taste

½ cup dry white wine

½ cup beef stock

2 Tbsp smooth apricot jam

3 Tbsp freshly squeezed lemon juice

2 ripe bananas

½ cup plain yoghurt

¼ cup cream

2 egg yolks

a pinch of baking powder

10 bay leaves

thin slices of lemon

20 whole almonds, toasted

Fruit compote

½ cup port

½ cup rooibos tea

3 Tbsp brown sugar

1 piece stick cinnamon

10 dried apple rings

10 dried sweet peaches

10 dried apricots

10 dried prunes

10 dried pears

Bobotie with a fruit compote

Preheat the oven to 180 °C. Grease 10 ramekins with a diameter of 9 cm.

In a large saucepan, heat the sunflower oil and sauté the onions and garlic with the salt until the onions are transparent. Add the curry powder, turmeric, coriander, cumin and cinnamon and stir-fry lightly. Add the mince and stir-fry quickly so that all the flavours are well combined. Pour in the lemon juice just before the mixture starts to catch. Add the apple, lemon zest, chutney, breadcrumbs, soy sauce and pepper. Simmer, covered, over a low heat for about 30 minutes, stirring at regular intervals.

Pour in the wine and stock and mix well. Simmer for another 15 minutes until all the flavours have blended. Spoon the meat mixture into the ramekins until each is three-quarters full.

Mix the apricot jam with the 3 tablespoons lemon juice, then spread it over the meat mixture. Cut the bananas into thin rounds or horizontal strips and arrange over the top. Beat the yoghurt, cream, egg yolks and baking powder together, and divide the mixture equally among the ramekins. Garnish with a bay leaf, a slice of lemon and a couple of almonds. Bake for about 30 minutes until the topping has set, or is golden-brown and puffed out.

For the fruit compote, heat the port, rooibos tea, sugar, cinnamon and dried fruit in a small saucepan over a low heat. Stir gently until all the fruit is soft, then remove the cinnamon. Spoon some of the fruit mixture into each ramekin and drizzle over a little of the cooking syrup when ready to serve.

Serve the *bobotie* with rice, onion marmalade and lightly toasted sesame seeds.

TIP: If you prefer, serve the compote in a separate bowl for each person.

This trusty recipe never fails to impress. I have adapted it considerably over the years and usually serve it in ramekins at Alfresco Deli.

Serves 10–12

3 x tagliatelle (see page 187)
a handful of fresh flat-leaf
parsley, finely chopped
2 Tbsp basil pesto
balsamic reduction for
drizzling
freshly ground black pepper
to taste

Sauce

1.5 kg beef cubes and cuts
with marrowbones
2 tsp coarse salt
2 Tbsp butter
¼ cup olive oil
4 shallots, peeled and sliced
into rings
4 white onions, peeled and
sliced into rings
4 red onions, peeled and
sliced into rings
1 sweet red pepper, cut
into strips
2 cups chopped mushrooms
(any sort)
4 cloves garlic, peeled
and chopped
4 cups dry red wine
4 tomatoes, skinned
and chopped
2 tsp cayenne pepper
2 Tbsp dried mixed herbs
410-g can tomato-and-
onion mix
2 x 400-ml cans coconut cream

Caramelised onions

2 cups chopped red onion
1 cup chopped white onion
2 Tbsp brown sugar
1 Tbsp balsamic or grape
vinegar
¼ cup brandy
4 cloves garlic, peeled
and chopped

Tagliatelle with marrowbone sauce

First make the sauce. Season the meat with the salt, then heat the butter and oil in a heavy-bottomed saucepan and fry the meat until sealed and browned. Remove the meat.

In the same saucepan, fry the shallots, onions, red pepper, mushrooms and garlic until well browned. Return the meat to the saucepan and fry a little longer until everything is well combined.

Pour in the wine and simmer slowly, covered, for about 2 hours until the meat is almost tender (stir gently from time to time but do not allow the meat to disintegrate).

Add the chopped tomatoes, cayenne pepper, mixed herbs, tomato-and-onion mix to the meat sauce and simmer, uncovered, for a further 20 minutes to allow the flavours to blend. Pour in the coconut cream and simmer for another 15 minutes over low heat.

To prepare the caramelised onions, cook the onions, sugar, vinegar, brandy and garlic in a saucepan over a low heat until caramelised and thick.

Cook the tagliatelle until *al dente*.

Serve the sauce over the tagliatelle and garnish with fresh parsley and some of the caramelised onions. Spoon a little basil pesto on top, then drizzle with balsamic reduction and grind over some black pepper.

My favourite Tradouw curry

± ¼ cup canola oil for frying

± 2 Tbsp butter

2 kg lamb (neck and knuckles)
   or 2 kg good-quality beef
   with marrowbones, cubed

2 cups buttermilk (soak the
   beef in it overnight)

4 white onions, peeled
   and chopped

2 red onions, peeled
   and chopped

4 spring onions, sliced

1 tsp coarse salt

4 cloves garlic, peeled
   and crushed

1 sweet green (for lamb) or
   red pepper (for beef), pith
   removed and thinly sliced

3 tsp finely grated fresh ginger

¼ cup medium smoked
   masala or hot curry powder

freshly ground black pepper
   to taste

6 cardamom pods, bruised

1 Tbsp ground cumin

1 Tbsp turmeric

1 tsp cayenne pepper

1 Tbsp ground coriander

¼ cup grape vinegar

2 cups lamb or beef stock

2 cups white wine (for lamb) or
   2 cups red wine (for beef)

1 cup dried apricots, diced,
   soaked in hot water
   and drained

2 Tbsp tomato paste

4 whole tomatoes, skinned
   and chopped

2 Tbsp white sugar

freshly squeezed juice of
   1 lemon

2 Tbsp apricot jam

4 Tbsp Bulgarian yoghurt

a handful of fresh coriander

In a large saucepan, heat the oil and butter, then fry the lamb or buttermilk-soaked beef until browned and set aside.

In the same saucepan, fry all the onions, salt, garlic and sweet green or red pepper, stirring continuously. Add the ginger, masala or curry powder, black pepper, cardamon, cumin, turmeric, cayenne pepper and coriander. Stir-fry for 1 minute.

Pour in the vinegar, stock and white wine (lamb) or red wine (beef), then add the apricots, tomato paste and tomatoes to the spicy mixture. Return the meat to the saucepan, cover and simmer for about 2 hours over a low heat, until the meat is tender. Don't stir too vigorously to ensure that the pieces of meat remain 'whole'. Mix the sugar and lemon juice together and as soon as the meat mixture starts to look dry, stir through the sugar-lemon mixture.

Just before serving, stir in the jam and yoghurt, and scatter over the coriander.

Serve with poppadoms (microwaved on high for 1–2 minutes until puffed) and basmati rice.

TIPS: Another option is to serve this curry with canned peaches bottled in ginger, chopped fresh mint and toasted mixed nuts. A simple tomato sambal made with small cubed tomato, chopped onion and parsley, or a carrot sambal made with grated carrot and ginger, is also delicious. My daughter Lena's favourite is a banana sambal of banana slices with Greek yoghurt and almonds.

Lamb, mutton or beef is suitable for this recipe. I often use chunks of beef, marrowbones or other beef cuts for a distinctive flavour and texture.

Serves 12

1 beef tongue, pickled
3 cups rooibos tea
1 onion, peeled and chopped
2 stalks celery, chopped
2 carrots, chopped
2 bay leaves
5 black peppercorns

Sauce
2 egg yolks, beaten
1 Tbsp apple cider vinegar
1 Tbsp brown sugar
2 Tbsp olive oil
2 tsp prepared wholegrain
  mustard
1 Tbsp freshly squeezed
  lemon juice
¼ cup mayonnaise
1 Tbsp honey
½ tsp ground cinnamon
1 tsp grated fresh ginger
salt and pepper to taste
1 bay leaf
¼ cup seedless raisins
a few capers
2 Tbsp toasted almond flakes
fresh dill or chives, finely
  chopped

Slaphakskeentjies
1 kg pickling onions, peeled
½ cup dry white wine
½ cup water
½ cup balsamic vinegar
½ cup dark brown sugar
1 tsp hot mustard powder
a pinch of salt
1 Tbsp olive oil
1 egg, beaten
1 Tbsp cornflour
a few curry leaves
½ tsp turmeric
2 capers

Sweet and sour beef tongue with *slaphakskeentjies*

In a pressure cooker, cover the tongue with the rooibos tea, add the onion, celery, carrots, bay leaves and peppercorns, and cook for 1 hour until the meat is soft. Remove the tongue and immediately plunge it into cold water. Make a small cut in the skin, then pull it off and cut away any muscle tissue as well. Return the tongue to the cooking liquid and leave to cool.

To make the sauce, beat the egg yolks in a metal dish positioned over boiling water. Add the vinegar, sugar and olive oil and mix well. Add the mustard, lemon juice, mayonnaise, honey, cinnamon, ginger, salt and pepper and beat continuously until the sauce starts to simmer. Remove from the heat and keep beating until it has thickened a little. Place back over the boiling water and add the bay leaf, raisins and capers and leave to simmer for a while to allow the flavours to infuse. Remove from the heat and remove the bay leaf.

Preheat the oven to 160 °C. Slice the tongue and arrange the slices in an ovenproof dish. Pour the sauce over the tongue and bake for 20 minutes. Remove from the oven, leave to cool, then scatter over the almonds and dill or chives on top.

For the *slaphakskeentjies*, boil the onions in the wine and water until soft. Drain, then transfer them to a serving bowl. Mix the remaining ingredients in a saucepan and heat slowly until the mixture starts to boil. Pour the hot mixture over the onions and leave to cool.

Serve the tongue and *slaphakskeentjies* with fresh, warm ciabatta (see page 55) or rye bread with which to mop up the tasty sauce!

Thank you to Peter Veldsman for his delicious 'slaphakskeentjies' (onion salad) recipe. I really can't imagine why they're called this. Do they look like 'floppy heels' (the direct translation from Afrikaans)?

Mabel's Tradouw Valley beef fillet

2 Tbsp prepared wholegrain
  mustard
¼ cup soy sauce
Maldon salt to taste
freshly ground black pepper
  to taste
2 kg beef fillet
¼ cup brandy
6 porcini mushrooms, chopped
6 oyster mushrooms, chopped
6 brown mushrooms, chopped
1 Tbsp finely chopped
  rosemary
2 Tbsp butter for frying
2 tsp beef stock powder
juice and zest of 1 lemon
½ cup cream
a large pinch of white pepper
green peppercorns, crushed,
  to taste
2 Tbsp grated Parmesan

Béarnaise sauce

¼ cup white wine vinegar
1 Tbsp chopped shallot
¼ tsp cracked black
  peppercorns
2 tsp chopped fresh tarragon
2 egg yolks
½ cup lukewarm clarified
  butter (ghee)
2 tsp chopped fresh parsley
Maldon salt to taste
cayenne pepper or Tabasco
  sauce to taste
freshly squeezed lemon juice
  to taste

Mix together 1 tablespoon of the mustard with the soy sauce, salt and pepper. Roll the fillet in this marinade mixture until covered. Place the fillet in a bowl, pour over any remaining marinade and refrigerate to marinate overnight.

Shake off some of the excess marinade mixture from the fillet, then fry in a hot griddle pan for about 15 minutes until sealed on all sides. The meat should still be tender and pink inside. Leave it to rest.

Mix the brandy and the remaining mustard with the leftover marinade, then marinate the mushrooms in this mixture for about 20 minutes. Remove the mushrooms and quickly fry them in the griddle pan used previously, along with the rosemary in a little butter until just sealed.

Transfer the leftover marinade-brandy mixture to a saucepan, then add the stock powder, lemon juice and zest, and the mushroom mixture. Bring to the boil over a high heat until reduced by half. Add the cream, more salt, pepper and green peppercorns, then simmer slowly until thickened.

Preheat the oven to 220 °C.

Just before serving, slice the fillet and place the slices in an ovenproof serving dish. Pour the sauce over the fillet, sprinkle with the Parmesan and warm through in the oven. In addition, serve the béarnaise sauce (below) on the side.

For the béarnaise sauce

In a saucepan, heat the vinegar, shallot, peppercorns and half of the tarragon until simmering, then allow to reduce until the mixture will yield about 2 tablespoons. Remove from the heat and transfer to a glass or stainless steel bowl. Add the egg yolks and beat for 1–2 minutes until light and frothy. Heat the egg and vinegar mixture for a minute, double-boiler style, until it thickens slightly. Remove the bowl from the heat and gradually add the clarified butter to the mixture (a couple of drops at a time), while beating continuously. If you add it too quickly, the emulsion won't hold. As the sauce starts to thicken, increase the tempo at which you beat it. When all the butter has been added, transfer the sauce to a clean bowl. Stir in the parsley and the remaining tarragon and season to taste with salt, cayenne pepper and lemon juice. The sauce should have a smooth, firm consistency. If it is too thick, adjust it by adding a few drops of hot water. Serve immediately.

I usually prepare the fillet in the morning, or even the day before guests arrive, and only heat it up once they are seated for dinner. It's delectable with a glass of Joubert-Tradauw R62 or Syrah and the béarnaise sauce!

Serves 4–6

± 500 g beef fillet, visible
 fat removed and cut into
 2.5 cm-thick slices
coarse salt to taste
freshly ground black pepper
6 cloves garlic (or more),
 peeled and crushed
¼ cup butter
1 Tbsp canola oil
1 large onion, peeled and
 thinly sliced
½ sweet green pepper, pith
 removed and cubed
½ cup dry white wine
2 tsp paprika
a pinch of ground cumin
1 Tbsp tomato paste
6 small ciabattas (see
 page 55)
fresh salad greens for serving
1 fresh ripe tomato, sliced, for
 serving
Tabasco sauce to taste
 (optional)

Chilli sauce

¼ cup seeded and finely
 sliced red chilli
¼ cup seeded and finely
 sliced green chilli
a pinch of cayenne pepper or
 to taste (optional)
2 Tbsp white wine vinegar
¼ cup olive oil
¼ cup water
a pinch of salt

Garlic beef fillet
with chilli sauce

First make the chilli sauce by mixing all the sauce ingredients with a hand-held blender, until smooth.

Arrange the fillet slices on a large wooden board and season with salt and pepper to taste. Rub a few pieces of the crushed garlic onto both sides of each fillet slice.

Melt half of the butter and the oil in a griddle pan over medium heat. Fry the meat quickly for about 2 minutes, turning once. Transfer the meat to a dish and cover with a lid.

Melt the remaining butter in the same griddle pan, add the onion and green pepper and fry until golden-brown. Transfer the onion mixture to the dish with the fillet. Pour the wine into the griddle pan. Add the paprika, cumin and tomato paste and scrape the bottom of the pan to incorporate the brown bits. Increase the heat to medium-high and allow the sauce to thicken slightly before returning the meat and onion mixture to the pan, heating for about 2 minutes.

Serve on crispy ciabattas or bread rolls with salad greens and slices of tomato, as well as a generous grinding of black pepper and a splash of Tabasco (if using), and a dollop of the chilli sauce.

Ideal for a Saturday in front of the TV if there's rugby to watch, or for a picnic in the Little Karoo veld.

Makes 8 medium pies

Shortcrust pastry
2 cups cake flour, sifted
½ cup cold butter, cubed
2 Tbsp iced water (or more if
    needed)

Filling
1 Tbsp canola oil
4 medium onions, peeled
    and sliced
salt to taste
½ cup chopped sweet
    red pepper
2 cloves garlic, peeled
    and crushed
10 button mushrooms,
    finely chopped
1.5 kg chicken portions (e.g.
    drumsticks and breasts)
6 allspice berries
3 whole cloves
6 blades mace
2 bay leaves
freshly ground black pepper
    to taste
½ –1 tsp Ina Paarman Lemon
    & Black Pepper seasoning
1 cup chicken stock
2 Tbsp sago, soaked in water
    until soft
½ cup dry white wine
½ cup brandy
1 egg yolk, lightly beaten
2 Tbsp freshly squeezed
    lemon juice
½ cup cream
4 hard-boiled eggs, shelled
    and sliced
egg wash (1 egg yolk mixed
    with a little milk)

Andreas's Tradouw chicken pie

To prepare the pastry, place the flour in a bowl and rub the cold butter into the flour with your fingertips until just combined to resemble bread crumbs. Add the iced water and compress the dough. Wrap in clingfilm, then refrigerate while you make the filling.

Preheat the oven to 200 °C.

In a pan, heat the oil and sauté the onions, salt, red pepper, garlic and mushrooms until lightly browned. In another saucepan, cook the chicken portions with the allspice, cloves, mace, bay leaves, Ina Paarman seasoning and stock until tender. Remove the hard spices and chicken pieces, debone the chicken and cut the meat into smaller chunks. Return the chunks to the onion mixture.

Add the softened sago to the chicken and onion mixture, followed by the wine and brandy and flambé. Simmer until the sago is transparent. Stir in the egg yolk, lemon juice and cream. Remove from the heat and leave to cool slightly.

Roll the pastry out thinly and cut out 16 circles with a diameter of about 7 cm. Work quickly to prevent the dough from drying out. Shape little leaves from the remaining pastry.

Line 8 small pie dishes with the pastry circles, then spoon in some chicken filling and place slices of hard-boiled egg on top. Cover each with another pastry circle and pinch the edges to seal. Make slits in the top layer of pastry, add a decorative pastry leaf and brush with the egg wash. Bake for 15–20 minutes until golden-brown.

Serve with yellow rice and a simple carrot salad made with grated carrots and Granny Smith apples, with fresh orange juice and pulp added.

Serves 6

2 Tbsp butter

2 Tbsp olive oil

1.5 kg beef fillet, cubed

2 cups roughly chopped
   red onions

1 cup chopped white onions

coarse salt to taste

1 sweet red pepper, pith
   removed and cut into strips

2–3 tsp chilli flakes or to
   taste

2 Tbsp chilli sauce

6 cloves garlic, peeled and
   finely chopped

½ cup tomato paste

1 bay leaf

juice of 2 lemons or to taste

20 black olives, pitted and
   halved

1 cup canned kidney beans

2 cups red wine

1 cup beef stock

freshly ground black pepper
   to taste

¼ cup cake flour and 2 tsp
   dried mixed herbs mixed to
   a thick paste with
   ¼ cup water

½ cup cream

Trinchado beef *bredie*

Heat the butter and oil together in a heavy-bottomed saucepan over a medium heat. Brown the meat, remove from the saucepan and set aside.

Sauté the onions, salt and red pepper in the same saucepan until the onions start to turn golden in colour. Add the chilli flakes, chilli sauce, garlic, tomato paste, bay leaf and lemon juice to the onion mixture. Boil for a few minutes until it is a fragrant sauce.

Return the meat to the saucepan and add the olives and beans. Pour in the wine and stock to cover the meat and bring to the boil over a medium heat. Reduce the heat to low, cover and simmer for about an hour. Add the pepper and the herb-and-flour mixture and stir. Cover and simmer for another 30–40 minutes until the meat is tender. Pour in the cream and simmer until slightly thickened.

This dish is usually served with potato chips or chunks of warm, fresh bread. It is extra delicious with a glass of white wine or a good port.

This is my version of this popular Portuguese stew, which has become a favourite in South Africa too.

Serves 6

2 Tbsp butter

½ cup canola oil

1.2 kg whole baby chickens
(200 g each or the smallest
you can find)

1 cup chopped bacon

½ cup coppa ham, cut
into strips

2 cups chopped white onions

4 red onions, peeled and
quartered

4 cloves garlic, peeled
and crushed

¼ cup brandy

2 cups red wine

1 cup chicken stock

¼ cup tomato paste

2 Tbsp finely chopped
fresh thyme

4 bay leaves

10 capers

1 cup cream

2 cups chopped porcini or
brown mushrooms

14 small pickling onions

1–2 handfuls fresh flat-leaf
parsley, chopped

freshly ground black pepper
to taste

Beate's coq au vin

Heat half of the butter and oil in a saucepan, then fry the chickens until browned on both sides. Remove from the saucepan.

In the same saucepan, stir-fry the bacon, coppa ham, white and red onions and garlic in the remaining butter and oil until lightly browned. Return the chickens to the saucepan. Add the brandy, flambé it and shake the saucepan until the flames die down.

For the sauce, mix together the wine, stock, tomato paste, thyme, bay leaves and capers. Add this to the chickens, cover and simmer for about 1 hour until tender.

Preheat the oven to 200 °C.

Add the cream, mushrooms and pickling onions to the chickens 10 minutes before the end of the cooking time and allow the cooking sauce to thicken. Transfer the chickens with all the sauce to an ovenproof dish and cover with a lid or aluminium foil. Bake on the middle shelf of the oven for 30 minutes, then remove the lid or foil and cook under the grill until the chicken skin blisters.

Sprinkle over the parsley and season with black pepper to taste.

Roast chicken with verjuice

Serves 8–10

¼ cup canola oil

olive oil to taste

16 chicken thighs

2 Tbsp chopped fresh thyme

2 Tbsp chopped fresh
   rosemary

coarse salt to taste

2 tsp lemon pepper
   (e.g. Ina Paarman Lemon
   & Black Pepper)

1 Tbsp dried mixed herbs

1 tsp mixed spice

¼ cup soy sauce

6 thin leeks, thinly sliced

5 artichoke hearts, chopped

16 green asparagus spears

10 capers

¼ cup freshly squeezed
   lemon juice

1 cup verjuice

a handful of pine nuts

¼ cup chopped fresh parsley
   or to taste

2 Tbsp finely chopped
   spring onions

Preheat the oven to 190 °C.

Heat the oil in a frying pan over medium heat and fry the chicken, thyme, rosemary and salt until browned. Transfer the chicken to a deep ovenproof dish and season with the lemon pepper, mixed herbs, mixed spice and soy sauce.

In the same frying pan, flash-fry the leeks, artichokes, asparagus and capers, adding a little lemon juice if it starts to catch. Pour in the verjuice and as soon as it starts to bubble, pour the mixture over the chicken, then cover.

Roast in the oven for about 40 minutes, then add the pine nuts and roast uncovered for another 10 minutes. Remove from the oven and scatter over the parsley and spring onions.

Serve with a potato bake made with cream and chopped green pepper.

The simplicity of this dish belies its tastiness.

Serves 6

2 onions, peeled and very
   finely sliced
2 cloves garlic, peeled and
   finely chopped
1 tsp finely grated fresh
   ginger
1 cup full-fat plain yoghurt
1 Tbsp masala spice
1 Tbsp tandoori or tikka spice
1 tsp paprika
1 green chilli, finely chopped
2 Tbsp chopped sweet
   red pepper
freshly squeezed juice of
   1 lemon
1 kg chicken portions (e.g.
   drumsticks and thighs)
2 cups uncooked basmati rice
2 Tbsp olive oil
1 tsp finely chopped garlic
4 spring onions, chopped
¼ tsp finely chopped green
   chilli (optional)
¼ tsp finely chopped red
   chilli (optional)
grated zest of 1 lemon
1 tsp mixed spice
½ tsp paprika
1 tsp chopped sweet
   red pepper
a handful of fresh coriander,
   finely chopped
freshly squeezed juice of
   ½ lemon
2 handfuls of fresh basil,
   shredded
freshly ground black pepper
   to taste

Tandoori chicken with basmati rice

Combine the onions, garlic, ginger, yoghurt, spices, red pepper and juice of 1 lemon. Make incisions in the chicken portions, then rub the marinade into the flesh. Marinate for 4–6 hours in the fridge or overnight.

Preheat the oven to 200 °C. Place the chicken in an ovenproof dish and roast for about 1 hour without adding any oil.

Boil the rice in salted water for 15–20 minutes, or until tender and light in texture.

Heat the olive oil in a saucepan and sauté the garlic, spring onions, chilli (if using), lemon zest, spices, paprika, red pepper and fresh coriander, but ensure that the mixture doesn't burn. When the flavours have blended, add the lemon juice, as well as the onion and garlic mixture to the rice, and stir through.

Transfer the rice to a serving dish and arrange the chicken portions on top. Garnish with the basil and grind over some black pepper. Serve with petits pois or a green salad.

This is undoubtedly my favourite stalwart for weekday evenings!

Serves 6

8 boneless chicken breasts
olive oil to taste
2 tsp garlic salt
freshly ground black pepper
    to taste
freshly squeezed lemon juice
    to taste
2 tsp finely chopped
    fresh thyme
2 tsp dried thyme
1 tsp chilli flakes or a mixture
    of fresh, chopped red and
    green chillies
16 fresh sage leaves
16 thin slices prosciutto or
    Parma ham
1 Tbsp finely chopped fresh
    rosemary
2 cups fine green beans
2 x tagliatelle (see page 187)
2 egg yolks, whisked
1 Tbsp melted butter
½ cup finely grated Parmesan
    or pecorino
a few shavings of Gruyère
toasted sesame seeds to taste
coarse salt to taste
2 Tbsp blanched almond
    flakes

Roast chicken wrapped in prosciutto

Preheat the oven to 200 °C.

Drizzle the chicken breasts with the olive oil, then season them with the garlic salt, black pepper, lemon juice, fresh and dried thyme and chilli flakes or fresh chilli. Press 2 sage leaves onto each breast, wrap each in 2 slices of prosciutto and secure with a toothpick. Arrange the chicken on a baking tray, sprinkle over the rosemary and roast on the middle rack of the oven for about 10 minutes on both sides (the meat should be cooked but still moist).

Bring a large saucepan with salted water to the boil, drop the green beans into the water for 3 minutes, then remove and rinse with ice cold water. Drain and set aside until needed.

Cook the pasta according to the instructions on page 187, until *al dente*, then drain and stir in the egg yolks, butter and Parmesan or pecorino.

Place the pasta on a large serving plate, place the chicken breasts on top and pile the green beans next to the chicken. Scatter over the Gruyère shavings and sesame seeds, season with more pepper and salt, and finally spinkle over the almond flakes.

Roast duck with orange, brandy and plum sauce

Serves 6

¼ cup orange liqueur
 (e.g. Cointreau)
¼ cup brandy
6 duck breasts (± 1 kg)
 with skin
coarse salt and freshly
 ground black pepper
 to taste
1 Tbsp butter
a few sage leaves to taste
2 Tbsp pine nuts
6 rashers bacon, chopped
a pinch of ground nutmeg
a handful of fresh thyme,
 finely chopped
2 tsp dried thyme
a handful of fresh parsley,
 finely chopped
juice and zest of 3 oranges
juice and zest of 2 lemons
½ cup brown sugar
½ cup apple cider vinegar

Plum sauce
1 cup prunes or fresh plums,
 quartered
½ cup dried figs, halved
3 Tbsp brown sugar
1 Tbsp honey
1 piece stick cinnamon
2 Tbsp brandy
½ cup chicken stock
2 Tbsp seedless raisins,
 soaked in white wine and
 well drained
½ cup of the duck's
 cooking liquid

Pour half the liqueur and brandy over the duck breasts, then leave to marinate overnight in the fridge. Season the duck with salt and pepper, and prick the skin with a toothpick.

Heat the butter in a pan and sauté the sage leaves, pine nuts and bacon together. Mix well with the nutmeg, fresh and dried thyme and parsley. Stuff this mixture under the skin of the duck breasts. Secure the skin with a toothpick if necessary.

Cut the orange and lemon zest into thin strips, then blanch in boiling water for 1 minute. Drain, plunge into cold water, drain again and set aside.

Preheat the oven to 200 °C.

In a frying pan, melt the brown sugar until caramelised. Add the vinegar and boil for 3 minutes. Pour in the remaining liqueur and brandy and set alight. Add the juice and prepared zest of the oranges and lemons and boil for another 3 minutes to make a glaze. Brush the glaze over the duck breasts and roast in the oven for about 15 minutes on each side. Baste the breasts often while roasting so that the skin is brown and crisp when done.

In a small saucepan, bring all the plum sauce ingredients to a boil. Continue boiling for about 30 minutes or until reduced by half. Stir well. Remove from the heat and decant into a gravy boat.

Arrange the duck breasts on a platter, thinly sliced if you prefer. Serve with the plum sauce and vegetables such as steamed broccoli and butternut, sprinkled with plenty of freshly squeezed lemon juice and ground black pepper.

TIP: As a garnish, flash-fry thinly sliced oranges in butter and scatter them over the breasts.

If you'd like to prepare a whole duck, cook it in a pressure cooker until tender, then glaze and roast.

Roasted Little Karoo lamb rack chops

Serves 8

16 lamb rack chops
½ cup chicken stock
½ cup dry white wine
⅓ cup butter
⅓ cup olive oil
2 onions, peeled and
    finely chopped
4 cloves garlic, peeled
    and crushed
¼ cup chopped spring onions
4 Tbsp roughly chopped
    fresh rosemary
1 cup crumbled feta with
    black pepper
6 anchovies
½ cup chopped pecan nuts
2 Tbsp prepared Dijon
    mustard
1 cup sourdough breadcrumbs
salt and freshly ground black
    pepper to taste
juice and finely grated zest
    of 1 lemon
1 Tbsp dried mixed herbs
1 tsp cayenne pepper
10 fresh basil leaves

Marinate the lamb rack chops in the stock and wine overnight, in the fridge.

Preheat the oven to 200 °C. Line a roasting dish with a large sheet of aluminium foil.

Heat the butter and olive oil in a saucepan, then sauté the onions, garlic, spring onions and rosemary until the onions are soft and translucent. Add the feta, anchovies, pecan nuts, mustard and breadcrumbs. Mix well and season with salt and pepper.

Pack the chops next to one another in the prepared roasting dish, fat-side up, and spoon the breadcrumb mixture in between the chops (but not on top of the fat). Sprinkle the meat with the lemon juice and zest, mixed herbs and cayenne pepper. Scatter over the basil leaves and roast for about 30 minutes, until the chops are golden-brown yet still pink inside. Finally, switch on the grill for a few minutes to crisp the fat.

This dish makes for a scrumptious Sunday lunch, or picnic in the Karoo veld.

Leg of lamb with a gooseberry glaze

Serves 10

2.5 kg leg of lamb, bone in
1 cup Bulgarian yoghurt
freshly squeezed juice of
    1 lemon
1½ cups dry red wine
salt and freshly ground black
    pepper to taste
10 cloves garlic, peeled
    and halved
2 Tbsp olive oil
2 Tbsp finely chopped fresh
    rosemary
2 Tbsp chopped fresh sage
4 tsp butter
1 cup chicken stock
1 cup canned gooseberries
    (reserve the juice)
2 Tbsp sherry vinegar
1 cup sliced shiitake
    mushrooms
1 cup sliced enoki or
    porcini mushrooms
1 cup cream
a large handful of fresh basil,
    roughly chopped

Gooseberry glaze
½ cup reserved gooseberry
    juice (see above)
2 tsp grated orange zest
2 tsp grated lemon zest
1 Tbsp brown sugar
2 Tbsp honey
1 Tbsp chutney
2 Tbsp brandy
coarse salt to taste

To marinate the leg of lamb, combine the yoghurt, lemon juice and 1 cup of the red wine. Pour the marinade over the meat and refrigerate overnight.

Preheat the oven to 200 °C.

Remove the leg from the marinade, then rub the surface thoroughly with salt and pepper. Make incisions in the meat and press the garlic halves deep into the slits. Heat the olive oil in an oven roasting dish on the stovetop over medium heat. Add the rosemary and sage and fry for 1–2 minutes. Add the butter and cook until foamy.

Place the leg of lamb in the roasting dish and shake the pan to coat the meat in the buttery mixture. Pour in the stock and roast, covered, in the oven for 30 minutes. Reduce the temperature to 150 °C and roast for a further 1½–2 hours, covered, until tender.

In the meanwhile, make the gooseberry glaze. Bring all the glaze ingredients to the boil and cook until reduced to a thickened consistency.

During the last 30 minutes of roasting, frequently brush the glaze over the leg. Finally, brown the roast, uncovered, under the grill of the oven. Transfer the meat to a platter and leave to rest in a warm place for about 30 minutes.

Place the roasting dish with the cooking liquid back on the stovetop, add the gooseberries, vinegar and remaining wine, then simmer until thickened. Add the mushrooms, cook for 2 minutes, stir in the cream and basil leaves and simmer until thickened.

Slice the meat and arrange the slices on the platter. Drizzle over the sauce and serve.

TIP: I serve this dish with vegetables such as cauliflower, steamed green beans with butter and flaked almonds, and crispy roast potatoes, and a garnish of fresh figs.

Grandma Katy's mutton tripe

Serves 10–15

1 kg sheep's offal (tripe and
    trotters), cleaned
500 g mutton neck
1 cup diced potato
½ cup coconut milk
½ cup balsamic vinegar
½ cup dry white wine
    (e.g. chardonnay)
1 Tbsp Maldon salt
1 tsp black peppercorns
12 new potatoes with jackets
½ cup apricot jam
2 tsp grated fresh ginger
5 cardamom pods, lightly
    bruised
1 star anise
1 tsp chilli powder
1 tsp ground cumin
½ tsp grated fresh nutmeg
2 tsp turmeric
a few threads of saffron
4 bay leaves

Cut the tripe into cubes. In a saucepan, pour a kettle of boiling water over the cubes, leave for a few minutes, then cook for about 20 minutes. Drain and rinse again in boiling water.

Add the trotters, mutton neck and diced potato to the saucepan with the tripe cubes. Cover with boiling water, add the coconut milk, vinegar, wine, salt and pepper, then simmer for 2 hours or cook in a pressure cooker for 45–60 minutes, until tender. The tripe should be tender, but the marrow should still be in the mutton bones.

When the tripe is tender, add the new potatoes and apricot jam. Mix the remaining ingredients together and stir this into the saucepan as well. Simmer for a further 30 minutes until the potatoes are soft. Add more apricot jam, vinegar, lemon juice and chilli poweder, if you like.

TIP: I serve the tripe with pot bread braaied over the coals, or lovely farm bread hot from the oven.

Tripe was a common dish when I was a child. We were sent to our rooms if we wrinkled our noses at the idea. Only later did I realise that tripe is an underrated dish, firmly established in Little Karoo culinary tradition. After I had eaten it in Paris, I realised it is also a French dish ('tripes'), and considered a delicacy! This version was inspired by Dine van Zyl.

Rolled leg of lamb roast

2 kg leg of lamb, deboned
coarse salt and freshly ground
   black pepper to taste
1 Tbsp dried thyme
5 cloves garlic, peeled and
   finely chopped
1 Tbsp grated lemon zest
¼ cup canola oil
¾ cup finely chopped dates
¼ cup butter
1 cup baby spinach or
   bok choy
4 tsp chopped spring onions
3 Tbsp finely chopped
   fresh rosemary
2 Tbsp chopped fresh thyme
2 Tbsp pine nuts, toasted
12 raw unsalted cashew nuts,
   finely chopped
¼ cup walnuts, finely
   chopped (optional)
1 round of feta with black
   pepper, crumbled
15 dried apricots, chopped
   and soaked in port
2 tsp finely chopped chillies
10 pitted black olives,
   chopped

Score a diamond pattern into the fatty side of the leg, then rub the salt, pepper, dried thyme, half of the garlic, lemon zest and oil into the fatty meat. Turn the leg over and, using a sharp knife, make about 10 incisions of 1 cm-deep in the meat. Stuff pieces of date into each slit.

Melt 2 tablespoons of the butter in a frying pan, sauté the spinach, spring onions, half of the rosemary and fresh thyme for about 1 minute. Reduce the heat and stir in all the nuts, feta, apricots, chillies and olives. Leave to cool. Spread the filling over of the meat, leaving a small clear border, then roll up the meat and tie with kitchen twine or place it in a meat net. Don't tie it too tightly – just enough to retain the shape of the roll. Wrap the meat in clingfilm and leave to rest in the fridge for about 3 hours.

Remove the meat from the fridge a few hours before you roast it and leave it to return to room temperature.

Preheat the oven to 200 °C.

Heat the remaining butter in an oven roasting dish on the stovetop and brown the lamb roll on all sides, together with the remaining rosemary, fresh thyme and the remaining garlic. Cover the dish and roast in the oven for 1 hour. Shake the pan lightly, turn the lamb over and roast for a further 20 minutes, uncovered, until browned but still pink inside. Leave the meat to rest before slicing it.

TIPS: Do the preparation for the lamb the day before it's roasted, and the roasting a few hours before your guests arrive. I make a brown sauce with mushrooms and the leftover pan jucies. Serve with sliced vegetables roasted with olive oil, fresh rosemary and coarse salt, as well as roast potatoes. Instead of a brown sauce, you could serve it with a tarragon sauce (see page 40).

Smoked leg of pork in phyllo, with honey and mustard

Serves 12

2 kg smoked leg of pork,
  soaked in cold water
  overnight and rinsed
1 Tbsp runny honey
1 Tbsp brown sugar
2 Tbsp mustard powder
2 tsp prepared hot mustard
1 tsp Worcestershire sauce
1 tsp tomato purée
1 tsp balsamic vinegar
± 15 whole cloves
500 g (± 12 sheets) phyllo
  pastry
3 Tbsp melted butter
sesame seeds for sprinkling
  (optional)

Mustard sauce
2 Tbsp butter
1 Tbsp chopped fresh thyme
1 Tbsp prepared hot mustard
2 Tbsp cake flour, sifted
¼ – ½ cup milk or sour cream

Drain the leg and rinse with cold water, then place it in a large saucepan with enough fresh water to cover the meat. Bring to the boil, reduce the heat, cover and simmer for about 1 hour.

Meanwhile, make a glaze by mixing together the honey, sugar, powdered and prepared mustard, Worcestershire sauce, tomato purée and vinegar.

Preheat the oven to 200 °C.

Remove the pork from the saucepan and drain again. Cut away the skin, but leave a generous layer of the fat. Press the whole cloves into the fat, then spread the glaze over the meat. Leave to cool slightly. Roast in the oven for about 1 hour until cooked. Reduce the temperature to 160 °C as soon as the fat starts to burn. Remove the pork from the oven, but leave the oven on. Place the meat on a wooden board to cool.

Make the mustard sauce by heating the butter over a medium heat, add the thyme and cook until softened. Slowly whisk in the mustard and flour. Gradually add the milk or sour cream, whisking continuously until it forms a smooth white sauce.

Brush each sheet of phyllo pastry with the melted butter. Line the bottom of an ovenproof dish with 4 sheets of phyllo. Slice the pork, then arrange the slices on top of the pastry, spooning the mustard sauce between the slices, but not over the fat. Fold the edges of the sheets of phyllo over the pork. Place another 4 sheets of buttered phyllo on top of the meat, tucking the edges underneath the bottom layers of pastry. 'Drape' the remaining 4 sheets of phyllo over the top, in a wave pattern (see photo opposite). Sprinkle over sesame seeds (if using), then bake on the middle rack of the oven for 20–30 minutes until golden-brown.

Slice through the phyllo and serve with roast potatoes and whole peeled carrots (quickly steamed, then fried in ginger and butter), as well as a fresh pineapple salad.

Varenka's rolled leg of pork

Serves 6–8

1 Golden Delicious apple, peeled, cored and grated

1 tsp grated fresh ginger

3 Tbsp water

1.5 kg leg of pork, deboned and butterflied

salt and freshly ground black pepper to taste

1 cup baby spinach

⅓ cup crumbled blue cheese

¼ cup grated frozen Brie or mozzarella (optional)

1 tsp paprika

1 tsp cayenne pepper

¼ cup olive oil

2 Tbsp freshly squeezed lemon juice

Onion spread

¼ cup butter

4 red onions, peeled and sliced

½ cup sage leaves

1 cup finely sliced porcini or brown mushrooms

100 g coppa ham, finely sliced

¼ cup soft brown sugar

¼ cup balsamic vinegar

coarse salt and freshly ground black pepper to taste

To prepare the onion spread, heat the butter in a large saucepan over medium heat then sauté the onions, sage, porcini or brown mushrooms and coppa ham until soft. Stir in the brown sugar, balsamic vinegar, salt and pepper. Reduce the heat and gently simmer the mixture for 30 minutes until caramelised. Set aside and leave to cool.

Make the apple mousse by heating the apple, ginger and water in a small saucepan over a medium heat. Simmer until soft and reduced to about a quarter of a cup.

Preheat the oven to 160 °C. Grease an ovenproof dish.

Season the pork with salt and pepper. Spread the spinach over the meat, followed by the onion spread, blue cheese and Brie or mozzarella (if using), apple mousse, paprika and cayenne pepper (leaving a border of about 1.5 cm clear). Roll up the pork and tie with kitchen twine.

Place the roll in the prepared dish, drizzle with the olive oil and lemon juice, then roast for about 1 hour, placing it under the top element of the oven for the last 10 minutes for a crisp finish.

If you like, serve with roasted sweet potato wedges, butternut or unpeeled pumpkin slices (roasted in the oven with olive oil, ground cinnamon, ground ginger, honey and some apple chutney until done).

My sister, Varenka, discovered this recipe on Huisgenoot magazine's website and tried it – it was a hit! I adapted it slightly for a unique flavour. Since then, I have become a fan of the website as a source of inspiration for new dishes.

Serves 8–10

Filling

12 black peppercorns
12 juniper berries
10 whole cloves
800 g venison, cut up (with bones)
600 g lamb or pork rib cutlets
3 bay leaves
3 tsp mixed spice
salt and freshly ground black pepper to taste
¼ cup red wine vinegar
1 cup beef stock
½ cup butter
2 large onions, peeled and chopped
2 cloves garlic, peeled and chopped
1½ cups diced streaky bacon
1 cup chopped brown mushrooms
2 stalks celery, chopped
2 tsp grated fresh ginger
1 tsp chopped fresh chilli
3 cups venison stock (from cooking liquid)
½ cup port
¼ cup freshly squeezed lemon juice
1 cup finely chopped dates
¼ cup tomato paste
2 Tbsp garlic salt
1 tsp freshly ground black pepper
¼ cup balsamic vinegar
½ cup pitted and quartered prunes

Pastry

500 g phyllo pastry
melted butter for brushing
a handful of garlic chives

Quince jelly

2 cups syrup from quince preserve
1 cup sugar
star anise
1 Tbsp gelatine powder

Little Karoo venison parcels

To make the quince jelly, heat the quince syrup, sugar and star anise in a saucepan over a low heat until the sugar has dissolved. Remove the star anise. Add the gelatine to a little lukewarm water and leave to sponge. When ready, whisk the gelatine into the syrup mixture. Pour the mixture into 8–10 ramekins and refrigerate for a few hours until set.

For the filling, use a pestle and mortar to grind the peppercorns, juniper berries and whole cloves until fine. Add the mixture, along with the venison and lamb or pork ribs, bay leaves, mixed spice, salt and pepper, vinegar and beef stock to a pressure cooker and cook until tender. Debone the meat (discarding the bones) and remove the spices, but reserve the cooking liquid until needed.

In a large, deep pan, heat the butter then brown the onions, garlic, bacon and mushrooms. Add the deboned meat, celery, ginger, chilli, venison cooking liquid, port, lemon juice, dates, tomato paste, garlic salt, pepper, vinegar and prunes. Stir while cooking, until the liquid has reduced enough for the filling not to be over-sauced when wrapped in the pastry.

Preheat the oven to 160 °C. Grease a baking tray.

Brush all the sheets of phyllo pastry (there should be 8–12) with melted butter, then cut each sheet into 4 squares. Stack 4 squares on top of one another in a star formation. Repeat with the remaining squares. Cover with a damp cloth to prevent the stacks from drying out.

Spoon about 2 tablespoons of filling into the centre of each phyllo stack. Draw the corners together and twist to form parcels. Dip the ends of the chives in boiling water, then tie a chive 'strand' around the neck of each parcel. Brush the ends of the pastry with more melted butter.

Arrange the parcels on the prepared baking tray and bake for about 10 minutes on the middle rack of the oven until pale golden-brown and crisp.

TIP: Serve each venison parcel with a ramekin of quince jelly, brown rice, whole fine green beans, mange tout, chives and brussel sprouts fried in butter and topped with toasted almond flakes.

2 kg ostrich fillet, cut into
    large cubes
3 Tbsp butter
2 Tbsp canola oil (if needed)
125 g bacon, chopped
125 g chorizo, sliced
4 cloves garlic, peeled
    and crushed
4 red onions, peeled and
    coarsely chopped
1 leek, chopped
½ tsp ground cloves
2 tsp chopped fresh thyme
    or to taste
2 tsp chopped fresh rosemary
    or to taste
500 g mixed mushrooms,
    sliced
2 cups pickling onions
1 Tbsp brown onion soup
    powder
1½ cups sour cream

Marinade

2 Tbsp olive oil
3 Tbsp balsamic vinegar
3 Tbsp freshly squeezed
    lemon juice
2 onions, peeled and finely
    chopped
2 tsp finely chopped fresh
    rosemary
1 tsp ground cloves
1 tsp ground nutmeg
2 star anise
½ cup beef or vegetable
    stock
1½ cups port
½ cup fresh or frozen
    cranberries
2 Tbsp dark brown sugar
salt and freshly ground black
    pepper to taste

The Jonkers' ostrich goulash with port

To make the marinade, mix together the olive oil, vinegar, lemon juice, onions, rosemary, cloves, nutmeg, star anise, beef or vegetable stock, port, cranberries, sugar, salt and pepper. Place the ostrich into a large dish and pour over the marinade mixture. Refrigerate overnight.

Heat the butter and oil in a large saucepan over a medium heat, then sauté the bacon, chorizo, garlic, red onions and leek. Add the ostrich cubes and the marinade. Add the cloves, thyme and rosemary, then simmer, covered, for 2 hours. Add the mushrooms, pickling onions and soup powder. Cook for a further 15 minutes or until the onions are tender. Stir in the sour cream and cook uncovered until the sauce has thickened. Serve with basmati rice.

TIP: Poach quinces or guavas in red muscadel and serve them with the goulash.

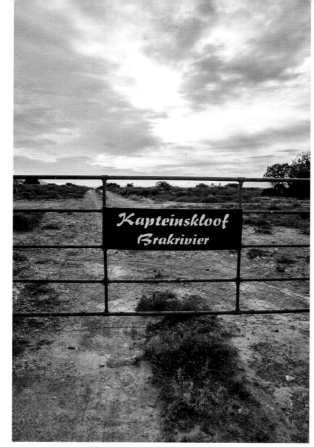

Venison *bredie* with prunes

Serves 8

¼ cup canola oil

500 g rindless bacon, finely chopped

3 large onions, peeled and chopped

a few cloves of garlic to taste, peeled and crushed

250 g brown mushrooms, sliced

2 kg venison, cut into large cubes

¼ cup tomato paste

salt and pepper to taste

2 cups prunes, pitted and quartered

1 cup water

2 cups red muscadel

1 piece stick cinnamon

Heat the oil in a heavy-bottomed saucepan. Fry the bacon until crispy, then add the onions, garlic and mushrooms and sauté until the onions are translucent. Add the venison cubes and fry over a high heat until the meat starts to brown.

Stir in the tomato paste with a little salt and pepper, then add the prunes, water, wine and cinnamon. Simmer, covered, for 2–3 hours or until the meat is tender. After about 1 hour, check that there is enough liquid in the saucepan, adding extra water if necessary. When the meat is tender, remove the lid and cook until the liquid has thickened.

Serve with samp and a green salad.

This dish is a delicious combination that you'll want to cook again and again. I first enjoyed it at the home of Annette le Roux, my long-time Little Karoo friend.

Serves 4–6

½ cup pesto (your choice)

½ cup mayonnaise

1 kg venison and beef
  mince, mixed

2 tsp dried mixed herbs

¼ cup olive oil

2 tsp mustard powder

2 Tbsp Worcestershire sauce

2 Tbsp tomato sauce

coarse salt and freshly ground
  black pepper to taste

¼ cup canola oil

cayenne pepper to taste

6 small ciabattas (see
  page 55), sliced open

a handful of butter lettuce
  leaves

6 slices white or strong Dutch
  cheese (your choice)

Tomato relish

2 cups whole cherry tomatoes

2 Tbsp soy sauce

2 Tbsp brown sugar

½ cup red wine vinegar

a handful of fresh basil, torn

coarse salt to taste

Onion relish

¼ cup butter

1 white onion, peeled and
  sliced

1 red onion, peeled and sliced

1 clove garlic, peeled and
  finely chopped

1 Tbsp cubed sweet red
  pepper

a pinch of coarse salt

The famous Alfresco Deli burger

First prepare the relishes and set aside until needed. For the tomato relish, submerge the cherry tomatoes in a bowl of boiling water for about 5 minutes, then skin them. Place the tomatoes, soy sauce, sugar, vinegar, basil and salt in a saucepan and cook over a medium heat until the mixture becomes a thickish relish. Remove from the heat.

For the onion relish, heat the butter in a large, non-stick pan over a medium heat. Sauté the onions, garlic, red pepper and salt for about 5 minutes. Remove from the heat.

Combine the pesto and mayonnaise until well mixed and refrigerate until needed.

To make the burger pattties, mix the mince with the dried mixed herbs, olive oil, mustard, Worcestershire sauce, tomato sauce, salt and pepper. Wet your hands, pinch off bits of the mixture, shape into balls then flatten slightly.

Heat the canola oil in a griddle pan over a medium to high heat and fry the burger patties for 4–5 minutes per side, until cooked but still slightly pink inside. Remove the patties from the pan and sprinkle them with cayenne pepper and salt.

Spoon a teaspoon of the onion relish onto each ciabatta bottom half, followed by a lettuce leaf, a slice of cheese, a patty, some pesto mayonnaise and finally a teaspon of tomato relish. Top with the other half of each ciabatta.

TIP: At my Alfresco Deli, I also serve these burgers with hummus, rocket leaves, thinly sliced fried brinjal and butternut, onion marmalade and the homemade tomato relish.

On the coals

Our fruit and wine farm is located in a region rich in beauty and character, and one in which food and wine are inseparable. The wonderful weather provides a perfect backdrop for entertaining friends and family *alfresco* style at long tables groaning with delicious food. Meals in the veld are a regular occurrence, especially around the braai, where we enjoy dishes straight from the fire. I don't provide instructions for preparing a braai as everyone has their favourite method and choice of wood, gas or kettle braai.

Serves 6

6 wooden sosatie skewers
  soaked in cold water for
  30 minutes
500 g lamb and beef mince
  mixed
a handful of fresh dill, finely
  chopped
2 tsp finely chopped fresh
  mint
2 tsp dried mint
2 tsp ground cumin
1 tsp turmeric
1 tsp cayenne pepper
1 Tbsp ground coriander
1 tsp dried chilli flakes
  (optional)
1 fresh green chilli, seeded
  and finely chopped
410-g can chickpeas, rinsed,
  drained and roughly
  mashed
1 red onion, peeled and
  finely cubed
3 Tbsp olive oil, plus extra
  for brushing
1 egg
a little cake flour for rolling
  the balls
2 Tbsp freshly squeezed
  lemon juice for drizzling
canola oil for frying
1 large unpeeled brinjal,
  sliced
1 Tbsp finely grated Parmesan

Beef, lamb and chickpea koftas with brinjal slices

In a bowl, combine the mince with the dill, fresh and dried mint, cumin, turmeric, cayenne pepper, coriander, chilli flakes (if using), green chilli, chickpeas and onion. Stir through the olive oil and egg. Wrap the mixture securely in clingfilm and refrigerate overnight.

Shape the meat mixture into 12 balls, each with a diameter of 4 cm, and roll them in flour. Place 2 balls on each skewer then reshape the balls into 'sausages' (koftas) around the skewers. Put the skewers in the freezer for about 1 hour, until set, but the meat shouldn't freeze.

Brush the koftas with olive oil and drizzle over lemon juice while slowly braaiing over medium coals until cooked.

Drizzle the canola oil over the brinjal slices and leave to stand until the oil has been absorbed. Braai over medium coals until soft. Sprinkle Parmesan over the brinjal slices and serve with the koftas.

TIP: You could use the meatballs as a filling in pita bread (see page 186) with fried onions and tzatziki or with sheet music bread (see page 52).

Delicious as a snack while waiting for the slower-to-braai dishes.

Klein Tradouw lamb or kudu liver in caul fat

Serves 6

18 squares caul fat
(± 6 x 6 cm each)
(a specialist butcher will
be able to supply this)
1 large onion, peeled and
finely chopped
1 tsp finely chopped garlic
1 tsp finely chopped fresh
rosemary
± 750 g lamb or kudu liver,
roughly chopped
1 slice molasses bread (see
page 56), finely crumbled
½ tsp ground cloves
½ tsp ground coriander
½ tsp ground nutmeg
finely chopped fresh parsley
to taste
salt and pepper to taste

Soak the caul fat in warm water for about 30 minutes. Drain.

In a frying pan, sauté the onion, garlic and rosemary, then leave to cool completely. Combine the liver with the onion mixture, bread crumbs, cloves, coriander, nutmeg, parsley, salt and pepper.

Spoon a tablespoon of the liver mixture onto each square of caul fat, then fold the fat around the liver and secure with a toothpick if necessary. Arrange the parcels on a braai grid (or in a heavy-bottomed saucepan).

When the coals are low, braai the meat (or fry on the stove top over a low heat) until browned and crispy (most of the fat will cook away).

Serve with hot mustard and fresh ciabatta (see page 55) with butter.

TIP: Ensure that you braai the parcels over a very low heat, otherwise they will burst open.

Klein Tradouw is a neighbouring farm. They regularly serve these to guests with a glass of cold chardonnay.

Tradouw leg of lamb on the fire

Serves 6–8

± 10 anchovies, chopped

2 Tbsp anchovy oil

10 black olives, pitted and
    finely chopped

4 cloves garlic, peeled and
    finely chopped

3 Tbsp chopped fresh thyme

2 Tbsp chopped fresh
    rosemary

½ cup Bulgarian yoghurt

freshly squeezed juice of
    1 lemon

2 kg leg of lamb, deboned
    and butterflied

½ cup red wine

freshly ground black pepper
    to taste

¼ cup olive oil

Combine the anchovies with the anchovy oil, olives, garlic, thyme, rosemary and yoghurt. Flavour the mixture with half of the lemon juice, then massage the mixture over the leg of lamb. Pour over the red wine and grind over pepper. Marinate in the fridge overnight.

When the coals on the fire are medium-hot, remove the leg from the fridge (but reserve the marinade for later use) and sear the meat, approximately 5 minutes per side, until well browned. Move the meat to a cooler section of the coals, or leave the coals to die down slightly, then braai slowly for about 20 minutes on each side. The meat must be juicy and pink inside.

Pour the reserved marinade into a pan and leave to reduce over the coals, stirring from time to time.

Remove the meat from the coals and squeeze the remaining lemon juice over it, followed by the olive oil and plenty of black pepper. Leave to rest for 10 minutes before slicing the meat and spooning the reduced marinade over it.

Delicious served with a glass of sauvignon blanc or merlot.

Serves 6–8

± 1 kg mutton ribs

Marinade
1 Tbsp coriander seeds
1 Tbsp freshly ground
   rainbow peppercorns
2 tsp coarse salt
1 tsp white pepper
½ cup olive oil
2 tsp finely chopped fresh
   red chilli
2 tsp finely chopped fresh
   green chilli
2 tsp dried chilli flakes
2 tsp chopped fresh rosemary
1 tsp dried rosemary
1 tsp dried origanum

Mutton rib to melt your heart

To prepare the marinade, grind the coriander seeds, peppercorns and coarse salt until fine, using a pestle and mortar. Rub the mixture into the mutton rubs. Mix the white pepper, olive oil, red and green chillies, chilli flakes, fresh and dried rosemary and origanum together until combined. Marinate the meat in this mixture overnight in the fridge. Do not discard the marinade once the meat is removed.

Preheat the oven to 140 °C. Roast the ribs on an oven rack in a flat roasting pan for about 3 hours. The fat should be crisp and golden-brown and the meat should look almost like biltong. Prepare a fire and when the coals are medium-hot, braai the meat slowly until it is tender, yet crispy on the surface, all the while basting with the reserved marinade. Cut the ribs into small pieces.

TIP: Serve the ribs on a wooden board with potato wedges baked in cream, paprika and garlic, and green baby asparagus, quickly blanched and then topped with lemon butter.

Buy the fattiest rib you can find and ask your butcher to crack it for you and cut diamond shapes into the fat.

Braaied mutton neck

Serves 6–8

3 mutton necks, sawn
   lengthwise
4 sprigs fresh rosemary

Stock
2 large carrots, coarsely
   chopped
1 onion, peeled and coarsely
   chopped
2 stalks fresh table celery,
   coarsely chopped
6 sprigs fresh parsley,
   coarsely chopped
4 whole cloves
2 bay leaves
1 tsp salt
1 tsp black peppercorns
1 tsp coriander seeds
200 g mutton bones
   with meat
2 litres cold water

Braai sauce
1 cup canola oil
½ cup brown vinegar
¼ cup honey
1 tsp salt
1 tsp white pepper
freshly ground black pepper,
   to taste
¼ cup Worcestershire sauce
1 sprig fresh thyme, chopped

Place all the ingredients for the stock in a large saucepan and cook slowly over a medium heat until reduced to about 1 litre of stock. Strain through a sieve and set aside until ready to use.

Preheat the oven to 180 °C. Place the mutton necks in an oven roasting dish. Pour over the stock and scatter over the rosemary then roast in the oven for about 3 hours.

In the meanwhile, mix all the ingredients for the braai sauce together until well combined. Prepare a fire and when the coals are medium-hot, braai the roasted mutton necks for 3 minutes per side, while basting with the braai sauce, until crispy.

My thanks to Dine van Zyl for her recipe. Our guests enjoy a glass of cold Joubert-Tradauw Chardonnay with this dish.

Serves 12

12 pork chops with fat

Sweet and sour sauce

¼ cup soy sauce
¼ cup freshly squeezed
   lemon juice
¼ cup port
1 tsp Ina Paarman's Lemon &
   Black Pepper seasoning
½ tsp white pepper
freshly ground black pepper
   to taste
¼ cup Ina Paarman's Sticky
   Marinade
2 Tbsp Ina Paarman's Lemon
   Marinade
4 cloves garlic, peeled and
   crushed or finely chopped
1 tsp finely grated fresh ginger
1 each fresh red and green
   chilli, finely chopped
   (optional)
1 tsp dried chilli flakes
1 tsp cayenne pepper
Maldon salt to taste

Cabbage

1 Tbsp butter
2 Tbsp olive oil for frying
3 red onions, peeled and
   quartered
⅛ red cabbage, shredded
⅛ green cabbage, shredded
¼ cup brown sugar
2 Tbsp honey
¼ cup port
1 piece stick cinnamon
1 tsp finely grated fresh ginger
2 whole cloves
1 star anise
1 cardamom pod
grated nutmeg to taste
1 cup chardonnay or
   sauvignon blanc

Sweet and sour pork chops with cabbage

Combine all the ingredients for the sweet and sour sauce in a food processor until well mixed.

When the coals of the fire are medium-hot, braai the pork chops, basting regularly with the sauce.

To prepare the cabbage, heat the butter and oil in a large saucpan. Sauté the onions until browned. Add the remaining ingredients and simmer slowly, covered, for about 45 minutes or until the cabbage and onions are tender. Remove the lid and continue cooking until the sauce has reduced, but don't overstir so that the cabbage doesn't disintegrate.

Angela and Hans Brochetto from Montagu supply our pork. You could substitute pork ribs for the pork chops in this dish, which we enjoy with a glass of port by Peter Bayly of Calitzdorp.

Serves 6

6 x 200-g eland or
   ostrich fillets
¼ cup melted butter
coarse salt to taste
½ cup fresh or frozen
   cranberries
¼ cup port
3 Tbsp brown sugar
onion marmalade to taste
   (see page 78)
6 pieces brie, melted
a handful fresh coriander or
   thyme, torn
freshly ground black pepper
   to taste

Marinade

¼ cup Worcestershire sauce
¼ cup red wine
1 Tbsp fruit chutney
⅓ cup balsamic vinegar
2 Tbsp brown sugar
1 Tbsp honey
1 tsp salt
2 tsp grated lemon zest
¼ cup freshly squeezed
   lemon juice
¼ cup port
2 tsp dried oreganum
2 tsp dried thyme
2 tsp mild mustard powder
2 tsp crushed garlic

Oupa Jacobus's venison or ostrich fillets over the coals

To make the marinade, mix all the ingredients together. Marinate the fillets in the mixture overnight in the fridge.

Remove the fillets from the fridge (but reserve the marinade for basting) and bring to room temperature. About 10 minutes before braaiing, mix the leftover marinade with the melted butter and salt, until combined.

Prepare your braai and when the coals are medium-hot, place the fillets on a grid and braai for 3 minutes on each side while basting with the marinade. Set the fillets aside to rest (they will continue cooking from the residual heat).

In a saucepan, over the medium-hot coals, mix the cranberries, port and brown sugar together and cook until the port is reduced by half.

To serve, place each fillet in a pan and spoon over a teaspoon of onion marmalade followed by the melted brie, and a teaspoon of the cranberry and port sauce. Sprinkle with coriander or thyme leaves and grind over black pepper to taste.

Serves 6–8

2 large free-range chickens

2 Tbsp olive oil, or more to
taste

Stuffing

½ sweet green pepper,
pith removed and
chopped (optional)

1 fresh green chilli, finely
chopped

2 Tbsp finely chopped
spring onions

2 cloves garlic, peeled and
finely chopped

2 Tbsp finely chopped fresh
thyme or 1 Tbsp dried
thyme

2 tsp ground allspice

1 Tbsp coarse salt or Ina
Paarman's Lemon Pepper

¼ cup soy sauce

2 rounds feta with black
pepper , crumbled

4 Tbsp freshly squeezed
lime juice

Braai sauce

¼ cup butter

2 Tbsp finely chopped
fresh rosemary

3 cloves garlic, peeled
and crushed

½ cup freshly squeezed
lemon juice

2 tsp garlic salt

The Jouberts' farm chickens

Preheat the oven to 140 °C.

Place the chickens in an ovenproof dish. Mix all the stuffing ingredients together, then stuff into the cavity of the chickens. Pour the olive oil over the chickens. Roast, uncovered on a middle shelf of the oven, for 45 minutes (this reduces the braai time).

In the meanwhile, prepare the braai sauce by melting the butter in a pan and sauté the rosemary and garlic. Leave to cool, then stir in the lemon juice and garlic salt.

Prepare a fire so that the coals are medium hot for braaiing the chickens. Once the chickens have been removed from the oven, brush the braai sauce all over them and cover the ends of the bones with aluminium foil. Braai the chickens on a grid for about 15 minutes per side, until well browned.

TIPS: I serve the chicken with browned onions and tzatziki with feta and Peppadews. You could debone the chicken and serve it in tortillas with plenty of fresh herbs or crispy potato chips. If you like, you could roast and braai the chickens on a kettle braai.

I love braaiing whole chickens over the coals and you can bet on it that children will eat every morsel. But if there is any left, it's easy to divide this chicken into portions. It's delicious as a cold picnic dish the following day.

Serves 6–8

1.5 kg pork belly, washed
¼ cup sesame oil
salt and freshly ground black
    pepper to taste
2 apples, cored and
    thickly sliced
2 red onions, peeled and
    thickly sliced
4 pickling onions, halved
2 cloves garlic, crushed
½ cup chicken stock
¼ cup white wine
a few stems of bok choy,
    rinsed and halved

Marinade

½ cup soy sauce
½ cup chutney
½ cup freshly squeezed
    orange juice
zest of 1 orange
¼ cup freshly squeezed
    lemon juice
zest of 1 lemon
2 cloves garlic, peeled
    and crushed
1 Tbsp finely chopped
    fresh thyme
1 star anise
1 piece stick cinnamon or
    1 tsp ground cinnamon
    (optional)
1 tsp chopped fresh ginger
2 fresh red chillies, finely
    chopped
¼ cup brown sugar
2 Tbsp honey

Tradouw pork belly over the coals

Preheat the oven to 200 °C. Make sure the top element is switched on.

In the meanwhile, combine all the marinade ingredients in a saucepan, bring to the boil, then cook until it becomes a thick sauce. Set aside.

Dry the pork with paper towel, make incisions in the fat and rub the entire surface with the sesame oil. Season with the salt and pepper. Roast in the oven, fat side up, for about 30 minutes until the fat is browned. Remove from the oven and set aside.

In another pot, steam the apples, all the onions, garlic, chicken stock, wine and bok choy together until tender. Set aside to cool.

Prepare the fire, then place the semi-roasted pork on a braai grid over medium coals and braai slowly until crispy, turning regularly. When clear liquid starts to leak from the bones, start basting the pork with the marinade, and baste regularly until the meat is done to your satisfaction.

Leave the pork to rest before slicing it. Arrange on a platter topped with the apple, onion and bok choy mixture.

TIP: As an alternative, serve the pork with apple chutney, fried rice noodles and baby carrots fried in honey, butter and ginger.

*My brother-in-law Schalk is a magnificent cook
— he encouraged me to create this dish.*

Braaied spiced neck of pork with a cucumber salad

Serves 4

4 large (± 1 kg) pork
   neck steaks

Marinade
1 Tbsp chilli oil
1 Tbsp sesame or avocado oil
2 tsp ground cumin
2 tsp ground coriander
1 tsp ground cinnamon
1 tsp each salt and pepper

Cucumber salad
1 Tbsp white wine vinegar
2 Tbsp avocado oil
2 Tbsp castor sugar
1 medium cucumber, seeds
   removed and thinly sliced
2 Tbsp finely chopped fennel
3 Tbsp chopped fresh mint

Mix all the marinade ingredients together until well combined.

Rub the marinade into the steaks, reserving the leftover for basting.

Prepare a fire and when the coals are hot, braai the pork, regularly turning and basting with the reserved marinade. The steaks must be brown, but not overcooked. Remember that the meat will continue to cook while it rests.

To prepare the cucumber salad, mix the vinegar, avocado oil and sugar together to make a dressing. Add the cucumber slices, fennel and mint to the dressing and marinate for 10–15 minutes. Serve the salad with the pork.

TIP: Lime chutney is delicious with this dish (see page 188).

1–2 pheasants, cleaned

1–2 carrots, roughly chopped

1 onion, chopped

2 bay leaves

¼ cup soft butter

3 Tbsp olive oil, plus more
    when necessary

8 chicken thighs

2 Tbsp chicken spice

1 cup chopped (2-cm pieces)
    chorizo, skin removed

1 cup cubed coppa ham

1 cup chopped bacon

8 pickling onions

4 cloves garlic, peeled and
    finely chopped

a few sprigs of thyme

1 Tbsp chopped fresh rosemary

1 sweet green pepper, pith
    removed and sliced

3 cups chopped porcini or
    brown mushrooms

2 cups dry white wine

1 cup chicken stock

1 cup freshly squeezed
    lemon juice

½ cup port

2 x 410-g cans butter beans,
    drained and rinsed

2 Tbsp chopped spring onions

2 tsp ground mixed spice

1 tsp grated fresh ginger

1 Tbsp mixed herbs

1 tsp white pepper

a few cardamom pods (optional)

coarse salt and freshly ground
    black pepper to taste

fresh basil, torn, or 2 Tbsp
    dried basil

Marinade

2 litres water

¼ cup salt

2 Tbsp olive oil

4 bay leaves

2 Tbsp sugar

½ cup freshly squeezed
    lemon juice

Pheasant and chicken *potjie* with porcini and white wine

To make the marinade, heat the water, salt, oil, bay leaves, sugar and lemon juice in a saucepan until the sugar has dissolved, then boil over a low heat for 5 minutes.

Cut the pheasant(s) into portions, place in a bowl and pour over the marinade. Marinate for 8 hours in the fridge, then remove the portions from the marinade (if they're left for longer than 8 hours, they will be too salty).

Place the pheasant portions, carrot/s, onion and bay leaves in a pressure cooker, cover with water and cook for about 1 hour until tender.

In the meanwhile prepare a fire. Over hot coals in a cast-iron pot, heat the butter and oil until frothy. Season the chicken thighs with the chicken spice and brown the thighs and pheasant portions for 3–4 minutes on each side. Add the chorizo, coppa ham and bacon and fry for a further 3–4 minutes until brown. Add more oil, followed by the pickling onions, garlic, thyme, rosemary, green pepper and mushrooms, then fry for about 10 minutes, until the onions are soft and golden-brown.

Pour a little of the wine into the pot and scrape the bottom of the pot to loosen all the bits. Add the stock, lemon juice, port, remaining wine, butter beans, spring onions, the spices and herbs, as well as the salt and pepper (the liquid should half-fill the pot). Simmer, covered, for 2 hours, or until the pheasant and chicken pieces are tender and the sauce is aromatic and thickened.

Remove the pot from the heat and leave the meat to rest in a warm place for 15–20 minutes – do not skip this step! Skim the excess fat from the sauce if the chorizo has rendered a lot of fat. Add a few fresh basil leaves or the dried basil to the saucepan.

Serve with creamy garlic potatoes or freshly baked bread.

Pheasant flesh tends to dry out quickly, so I use chorizo and coppa ham for extra fat and flavour. The butter beans are delicious because they absorb all the flavours of the meat, wine and herbs, and can be mashed into the sauce on one's plate. I first marinate the pheasants, then add the chicken to make the dish less 'wild'.

Serves 8–10

1.5 kg mutton rib, neck, tail
    and knuckles
1 tsp finely chopped fresh
    rosemary
12 pickling onions
1 large onion, peeled and
    finely chopped
1 tsp coarse salt
butter to taste
4 cloves garlic, peeled and
    finely chopped
2 tsp finely chopped ginger
1 litre chicken stock
½ cup soy sauce
½ cup freshly squeezed
    lemon juice
¼ cup balsamic vinegar
1 cup dry white wine
3 kg baby *waterblommetjies*
15 new potatoes
freshly ground black pepper
    to taste
1–2 handfuls of wild sorrel
    (dock), picked in the veld
    and finely chopped, or
    2 Tbsp lemon zest
1 cup cream
2 Tbsp brown onion
    soup powder

Tradouw *waterblommetjie* stew

Prepare a fire and when the coals are medium-hot, place the meat and rosemary in a large cast-iron pan and brown the meat in its own fat. Remove the meat from the pan and set aside.

In the same pan, brown all the onions with the salt and butter. Add the garlic, ginger, meat, stock, soy sauce, lemon juice, vinegar and wine. Cover and simmer slowly for 1 hour. Add the *waterblommetjies* and potatoes to the pan, season with pepper and simmer, covered, for another 30 minutes.

Add the sorrel or lemon zest and simmer for a further 20 minutes, until the meat is very tender. Mix the cream and soup powder together, then stir it lightly through the contents of the pan for a creamy texture without mixing everything together.

Serve with crushed wheat and roasted beetroot with feta and quinces.

TIP: To clean *waterblommetjies*, soak them in salted water for 30 minutes, then rinse thoroughly. To freeze them, place them in a colander after the salting and rinsing, pour over boiling water and drain. Pour iced water over them and drain again before storing in the freezer.

My children and I love floating on an inner tube on our farm dam and picking 'waterblommetjies' until we have a full bag. I enjoy the pungency of this recipe.

144

Serves 8

1 cup cake flour, sifted

1 Tbsp paprika

2 kg oxtail, cut into portions

¼ cup canola oil for frying

2 Tbsp butter for frying

50 g bacon

½ cup coppa ham, sliced

2 Tbsp finely chopped
   rosemary

2 white onions, peeled and
   roughly chopped

2 red onions, peeled and
   roughly chopped

1–2 sweet red peppers, pith
   removed and sliced

5 cloves garlic, peeled and
   crushed

10 porcini or brown
   mushrooms, sliced

1 stalk celery, finely chopped

2 bay leaves

2 pieces stick cinnamon

3 star anise

2 tsp ground cumin

¼ cup tomato paste

2 cups dry red wine

2 cups cherry tomatoes,
   skinned

1 cup beef stock

coarse salt and pepper
   to taste

6 ripe hard-eating white
   pears, cored and sliced into
   5-cm wide strips

1 cup cream

Little Karoo oxtail *potjie*

Prepare a fire.

Mix the flour and paprika together, then roll the meat in it until covered. When the coals are medium-hot, heat the oil in a No. 4 three-legged *potjie* and fry the bacon, coppa ham, rosemary and oxtail portions until sealed. Remove from the pot and set aside.

In the same pot, sauté the onions and red peppers until the onions are golden-brown, then add the garlic, mushrooms, celery, bay leaves, cinnamon, star anise and cumin, stirring until well combined. Stir in the tomato paste and wine, and cook until the liquid has reduced by half.

Add the tomatoes and stock, then return the meat and bacon mixture to the pot. Season with salt and black pepper. Heat to boiling point, then reduce the heat and cover. Simmer for about 3 hours until the meat is tender, adding wine if it becomes too dry.

Add the pears about 30 minutes before the end of cooking time – the pears should just poach and not disintegrate. Season to taste and thicken with the cream, stirring through gently, shortly before the end of cooking time.

Serves 6–8

¼ cup canola oil
800 g cubed stewing beef
    with marrowbones
3 white onions, peeled
    and chopped
2 red onions, peeled and
    chopped
2 cloves garlic, peeled
    and crushed
1 tsp coarse salt
1 sweet green pepper, cubed
2 tsp turmeric
2 tsp curry powder
1 Tbsp paprika
2 tsp cayenne pepper
1 Tbsp ground cumin
1 piece stick cinnamon
1 star anise
800 g tomatoes, skinned
    and finely chopped
¼ cup tomato purée
410-g can tomato-and-
    onion mix
± 8 dates, pitted and
    quartered
2 Tbsp Ina Paarman's Brown
    Gravy Powder
2 cups beef stock
1 cup dry red wine
2 cups dried brown lentils
chopped fresh coriander
    to taste
freshly ground black pepper
    to taste

Tradouw beef and lentil stew

Prepare a fire. When the coals are medium-hot, heat the oil in a heavy-bottomed pot and brown the meat well on all sides. Remove the meat from the pot and set aside.

In the same pot, sauté the onions, garlic, salt and green pepper until the onions are golden-brown. Stir in the turmeric, curry powder, paprika, cayenne pepper, cumin, cinnamon and star anise. Add the tomatoes, tomato purée, tomato-and-onion mix, dates, gravy powder, stock, wine and meat, and simmer for 2–3 hours until the meat is tender. Season to taste and stir in the lentils. Cook for a further 30 minutes until the lentils are soft.

Sprinkle over the coriander and grind over some black pepper before serving.

I love 'bredies' (stews), beans and lentils — they're my soul food!

Serves 6

canola oil to taste

6 large white onions, peeled and finely chopped

3 red onions, peeled and finely chopped

1 sweet green pepper, pith removed and sliced

1 tsp coarse salt

1 sheep's stomach (tripe), scraped clean and cut into small cubes

6 sheep's trotters, cleaned

1 kg sheep's neck, sliced

2 cloves garlic, peeled and crushed

2 cups whole dried apricots

2 cups chopped dried peaches

¼ cup curry powder

1 Tbsp Ina Paarman's Roast Onion Soup & Gravy Powder

¼ cup brown sugar

1 tsp chilli powder (optional)

freshly squeezed juice of ½ lemon

3 Tbsp balsamic vinegar

3 Tbsp tomato paste

freshly ground black pepper to taste

2 cups Old Brown Sherry

1 cup chardonnay

16 new potatoes

Grandma Matty's *potjie* of curried mutton tripe and trotters

Prepare a fire. When the coals are medium-hot, heat the oil in a large three-legged *potjie* and sauté the onions, green pepper and salt until the onions are transparent.

Add the tripe and trotters to the pot, then arrange the slices of neck, garlic, apricots and peaches on top. Mix together the curry powder, gravy powder, brown sugar, chilli powder, lemon juice, vinegar, tomato paste, black pepper, sherry and chardonnay, and pour the mixture over the top.

Simmer for about 4 hours until the meat is tender. If it starts to catch, add more wine. Add the potatoes after 3 hours of simmering time (1 hour should be sufficient for them to cook).

TIP: Serve with samp and beans, cooked with a packet of brown onion soup powder, enough water to cover and cubes of green pepper to taste. I usually cook this in a pressure cooker until tender. This *potjie* can also be served with freshly baked white bread and farm butter.

The first time I ate tripe with potatoes and a dark onion sauce, it was an unforgettable experience! This recipe has changed little over the years and is in memory of my grandma from Gordon's Bay.

Braaied peri-peri prawns

Serves 4–6

1 tsp hot red or green chilli
    paste
6 cloves garlic, peeled and
    finely chopped
¼ cup finely chopped fresh
    coriander
⅓ cup white wine or to taste
⅓ cup freshly squeezed
    lemon juice or white wine
    vinegar
⅓ cup olive oil
a pinch of chilli powder or
    ¼ tsp finely chopped fresh
    red chilli
800 g prawns, with shells
± 15 wooden sosatie sticks,
    soaked in water for 30
    minutes

Mix the chilli paste, garlic, coriander, white wine, lemon juice or vinegar, olive oil and chilli powder or fresh chilli together in a deep bowl. Add the prawns and marinate for about 30 minutes.

Prepare a fire. Thread the prawns onto the sosatie sticks. When the coals are medium-hot, braai the prawns for 2 minutes on each side until they are light pink and start to curl.

Serve with yellow rice, olive ciabatta (see page 55) and a hot chilli sauce.

TIP: I make a salsa from cubed papaya, mango, avocado, spring onions, feta, plenty of lemon juice, freshly ground black pepper, finely chopped fresh coriander and Tabaso sauce to taste.

These prawns taste so good when accompanied by a glass of chardonnay.

Sweet

This collection of desserts represents my 'memory food' – puddings and other 'sweets' that my grandmothers and mother made with so much love. I now make them for my own family to keep the tradition alive. I also enjoy satisfying desserts such as sago pudding, panna cotta and bread pudding, combined with typical Little Karoo elements. The creaminess of a rice pudding with citrus flavours take me back to the Sunday dinner desserts of my childhood.

Grandma Rina's creamy orange sago pudding

Serves 8–10

1½ cups sago, rinsed
2 cups cream
1 piece stick cinnamon
2 cups milk
½ cup coconut milk
½ cup freshly squeezed
   orange juice
½ cup white sugar
a pinch of salt
4 tsp grated orange zest
2 Tbsp butter
4 large eggs, separated
⅓ cup castor sugar
cinnamon-sugar for sprinkling

Preheat the oven to 180 °C. Grease a 2-litre volume baking dish.

Place the sago in a saucepan and add the cream, cinnamon, milk, coconut milk and orange juice. Simmer over a low heat for about 30 minutes, until the sago is transparent. Stir in the white sugar, salt, orange zest and butter, until the butter has melted. Remove from the heat and carefully remove the cinnamon stick from the mixture.

Lightly beat the egg yolks and stir into the sago mixture. Spoon the mixture into the prepared baking dish. Beat the egg whites until stiff, then slowly beat in the castor sugar. Spoon the meringue over the sago mixture and bake for about 25 minutes until set.

Sprinkle lightly with cinnamon-sugar and serve hot.

I cannot imagine life without my mom's hot sago pudding. This is my favourite version because of the lovely orange flavour. Serve during winter with a glass of sherry.

Tradouw panna cotta with lemon and rose or peach and walnut

Serves 6

Panna cotta

1 vanilla pod
2 tsp finely grated lemon zest
1 cup cream mixed with
   1 cup milk
½ cup castor sugar
6 fresh mint leaves
1 Tbsp gelatine powder
1 cup Greek yoghurt
¼ cup icing sugar, sifted
a pinch of salt

Lemon and rose syrup

¼ cup freshly squeezed
   lemon juice
⅓ cup castor sugar
2 tsp rose water
¼ cup water
2 Tbsp Butlers Strawberry
   Liqueur (optional)
thinly sliced strawberries and
   other red berries to taste
petals of 1 organic red rose
icing sugar for topping

Peach jelly and walnut topping

80-g packet peach jelly
   powder
2 Tbsp butter
12 slices fresh peach
2 Tbsp brown sugar
a handful of toasted walnuts,
   chopped
honey to taste
ground cinnamon

To prepare the panna cotta, split the vanilla pod and scrape out the seeds with the sharp point of a small knife. Place the seeds in a saucepan, over a medium heat, together with the whole pod, lemon zest, cream and milk mixture, castor sugar and mint. Stir until the sugar has dissolved, then bring to the boil. Reduce the heat and simmer gently for 10 minutes.

Sprinkle the gelatine powder over a little lukewarm water in a bowl and allow to sponge. Mix some of the warm vanilla mixture with the gelatine, then add this to the rest of the vanilla mixture and stir through. Strain the mixture to remove the vanilla pod and mint leaves, then set aside to cool slightly. Stir in the yoghurt, icing sugar and salt.

Rinse 6 ramekins (each with a capacity of 150 ml) with cold water and pour in the panna cotta mixture while the ramekins are still wet. Leave to cool completely, cover with clingfilm and refrigerate for 4–6 hours or overnight until set.

Turn out each panna cotta onto a side plate (dip the base of the ramekins in hot water for 5 seconds if they stick). Finish by adding one of the topping options below.

Heat the lemon juice, castor sugar, rose water, water and strawberry liqueur (if using) in a small saucepan over a medium heat. Stir until the sugar has dissolved, then bring to the boil. Reduce the heat and simmer until syrupy. Just before removing it from the heat, add a few of the sliced strawberries. Chop six of the rose petals finely and add to the syrup. Refrigerate until ready to serve.

To serve, spoon the syrup over the panna cottas and decorate with rose petals, strawberries, or other red berries and sift over icing sugar.

Make the jelly according to the packet instructions and fill the ramekins a quarter full, then refrigerate until set. When the jelly has set, top up the ramekins with the panna cotta mixture. Cover with clingfilm and refrigerate for 4–6 hours until set.

Half an hour before serving, melt the butter in a pan and fry the peach slices. Sprinkle over the brown sugar and continue frying until lightly browned and well caramelised.

To serve, top the panna cottas with the peach slices. Sprinkle with the chopped walnuts, a drizzle of honey and finally, some ground cinnamon.

Goat's milk cheese mini custards

Serves 4

1 cup fresh goat's milk
    cheese, at room
    temperature
¼ cup castor sugar
½ cup cream
3 large egg yolks
½ tsp vanilla essence or a
    few vanilla seeds
ground cinnamon for
    sprinkling
fresh mint, chopped

Red wine syrup

½ cup red wine
3 Tbsp green fig
    preserve syrup
3 Tbsp brown sugar
1 piece stick cinnamon or a
    pinch of ground cinnamon
a pinch of freshly ground
    black pepper
a few vanilla seeds
sliced fresh strawberries
    to taste

Preheat the oven to 180 °C. Place four ramekins in a deep ovenproof dish.

Mix together the goat's milk cheese, castor sugar, cream, egg yolks and vanilla essence or seeds for about 30 seconds until smooth. Divide the mixture among the ramekins, filling them to just over halfway. Pour hot water into the ovenproof dish to reach about halfway up the sides of the ramekins. Cover the entire dish with aluminium foil and bake for 15–20 minutes.

Remove the ramekins from the bain-marie and leave to cool to room temperature. They can be stored in the fridge for 2 days (but cover with clingfilm and bring to room temperature before serving).

To prepare the syrup, bring the red wine, fig syrup, brown sugar, cinnamon, black pepper and vanilla seeds to the boil and cook until the liquid has reduced by half. Remove from the heat, pour into a bowl and leave to cool. Add the strawberries and leave to stand for 1–2 minutes. Spoon the syrup and strawberries over the cooled custards in the ramekins, then sprinkle over a little cinnamon and chopped fresh mint.

Oven temperatures can vary and custard is notorious for its uncertain baking time. The best way to judge is to bake until the custard is just slightly wobbly and not completely set. If in doubt, rather remove it from the oven and keep covered; it should set while resting.

If you like, you could make the custard with half milk, half cream — it works well. I prefer using only cream because it results in the smoothest possible custard.

Our favourite French crêpes with orange sauce

Serves 8

1 cup flour, sifted
½ tsp salt
2 tsp baking powder
2 eggs
¼ cup canola oil
2 Tbsp white wine vinegar
2 Tbsp brandy
1 cup water (or more for a
  thin batter)
butter or oil for frying

Orange sauce
1 cup white sugar
½ cup freshly squeezed
  orange juice
1 star anise
¼ cup butter
1 Tbsp grated orange zest
1 Tbsp brandy (optional)
1 Tbsp freshly squeezed
  lemon juice

Beat the flour, salt, baking powder, eggs, oil, vinegar and brandy together until combined. Add the water, a little at a time to avoid lumps. Refrigerate the batter overnight or for at least 1 hour if time is limited, allowing it to rest and the ingredients to blend.

Heat a frying pan over a medium to high heat and melt a little butter or oil, just enough to cover the bottom of the pan lightly. Pour a third of a cup of batter into the centre of the pan, then tilt the pan until the batter has covered the entire surface. Fry for about 2 minutes, then flip the crêpe and fry for a further 1–2 minutes, until both sides are browned. The crêpe will be a little crisp around the edges and the centre will be brown or form blisters.

Remove the crêpe from the frying pan and place on a plate positioned over a saucepan of simmering water (to keep the crêpe warm), then cover with a lid. Repeat until you have used all the batter. After each 3 crêpes, add a little more butter or oil to the pan.

For the orange sauce, heat the sugar, orange juice and star anise in a small saucepan over a medium heat, stirring until the sugar has dissolved. Bring to the boil and cook until the mixture reduces and thickens. Stir in the butter, orange zest, brandy (if using) and lemon juice. Remove the star anise.

When the sauce is ready, first fold each crêpe in half, then fold again to form a triangle. Arrange the crêpes on a platter and drizzle over the sauce.

TIPS: I fill the crêpes with a teaspoon of dark chocolate spread or melted dark chocolate, or a slice of preserved fig, or fresh figs soaked in port, or a banana baked in brown sugar and butter with a teaspoon of caramel and cream to taste. Sometimes I even serve them with a ganache made from white chocolate and broken almonds before folding them into triangles. The basic ratio is 2 parts chocolate to 1 part cream. Heat the cream and chocolate (do not boil) until the chocolate has just melted, add the almonds, then pour it directly onto a sheet of baking paper and place in the fridge to set. Cut the set chocolate into triangles and place on top of the crêpes.

The crêpes should be paper thin. If the batter is too thick you will end up with farm-style pancakes instead of French crêpes!

**Makes a 25-cm
double-layer cake**

3¼ cups cake flour
4 tsp baking powder
8 eggs, separated
1 cup castor sugar
1 tsp ground cardamom
½ cup butter, melted

Praline
1 cup castor sugar
2 Tbsp water
½ cup mixed nuts

**Strawberry jam
filling**
1 cup whole-fruit
    strawberry jam
1 cup strawberries, chopped
½ cup castor sugar
1 star anise
1 piece stick cinnamon
2–3 tsp gelatine powder
½ cup lukewarm water
1 cup cream, stiffly whisked

Topping
½ cup soft butter
2 cups icing sugar, sifted
1 cup smooth full-cream
    cream cheese
1 tsp vanilla essence or seeds
    of 1 vanilla pod
white chocolate curls for
    decorating
organic rose petals (your
    choice of colour)

Mom's strawberry sponge cake with praline

Preheat the oven to 180 °C (switch on the fan, if available). Thoroughly grease two 25-cm cake tins.

Sift the flour and baking powder together. Do this three times in order to make sure the flour is well aerated.

Using an electric mixer, beat the egg yolks then add the castor sugar and cardamom. Beat at high speed for 8–10 minutes, or until thick and foamy. Using a figure-of-eight movement and a large metal spoon, carefully fold the flour mixture into the egg mixture. Gently fold in the melted butter. Whisk the egg whites until stiff, then fold lightly into the flour and egg mixture. Divide the batter between the two prepared cake tins. Bake for 20–25 minutes, or until golden-brown and cooked through. Turn out onto a wire wrack and leave to cool.

To prepare the praline, melt the castor sugar and water in a saucepan over a low heat. Tilt the pan, but do not stir, allowing the sugar to dissolve and caramelise. Gently stir in the nuts, then pour onto a silicone mat or a baking sheet sprayed with cooking spray. Refrigerate until set. Once set, break the praline into shards.

For the strawberry jam filling, heat the jam, strawberries, castor sugar, star anise and cinnamon in a saucepan, stirring until reduced to a spreadable consistency. Remove from the heat, then remove the star anise and stick cinnamon.

Sponge the gelatine over the lukewarm water. Stir the dissolved gelatine through the strawberry mixture until combined. Refrigerate until set. Spread a layer of the filling over the bottom cake layer, followed by a layer of whipped cream. Place the top layer of the cake over the cream.

To make the topping, whisk the butter until creamy, then add the icing sugar and continue mixing until pale yellow in colour. Mix in the cream cheese and vanilla essence or seeds until combined. Spread the mixture over the top and sides of the cake. Decorate the cake with the chocolate curls, shards of praline and rose petals.

Sofia's banana meringue muffins

Makes 12

200 g butter, melted
1 cup castor sugar
1½ cups self-raising flour
1 tsp baking powder
4 eggs, separated
1 Tbsp ground cinnamon
1 tsp mixed spice
1–2 ripe bananas, mashed

Meringue topping
2 egg whites
½ tsp bicarbonate of soda
¾ cup castor sugar

Preheat the oven to 180 °C. Line a 12-cup muffin tin with paper liners.

Cream the butter and castor sugar together in a large bowl. Sift the flour and baking powder into a separate bowl, then add the flour mixture, along with the egg yolks, cinnamon and mixed spice to the butter mixture. Beat with a hand mixer for about 3 minutes until smooth. Add the bananas and stir through lightly.

Whisk the egg whites until stiff peaks form, then fold into the batter, using a metal spoon.

Spoon the mixture into the muffin liners, filling them about three-quarters full. Bake for 20 minutes or until a metal skewer inserted into the centre of a muffin comes out clean. Remove from the oven and set aside while you make the meringue topping.

Increase the oven temperature to 230 °C.

To make the meringue topping, beat the egg whites in a glass bowl with a hand mixer until stiff peaks form. Still beating, add the bicarbonate of soda. Add a quarter cup of the sugar, beat, and repeat until all the sugar has been incorporated. Do not add too much sugar at once.

Fill a piping bag with the mixture, then pipe the meringue over top of each muffin. Return the muffin tin to the oven and bake for 5–10 minutes on the centre shelf, just until the meringue starts to brown.

I always enjoy recipes that are a little different, and because most children love banana bread, you can be sure that they'll love these muffins too!

320 g butter or baking
    margarine, plus extra
    for greasing
1 cup cocoa powder
1 cup castor sugar
2 x 80-g slabs dark chocolate
    (one with mint and one
    with nuts), broken
1½ cups cake flour
4 tsp baking powder
¼ tsp salt
8 eggs, separated
2 Tbsp vanilla essence
⅓ cup brandy
⅓ cup premade espresso
dark chocolate curls for
    decorating
4 whole preserved green figs
    and about ¼ cup fig syrup
4 fresh whole figs, halved, for
    decorating
rose petals for decorating
    (optional)
fresh mint leaves

Syrup

1½ cups white sugar
1 cup water
½ cup premade espresso

Icing

⅓ cup butter
2 x 80-g slabs dark chocolate
    with nuts or mint, broken
¼ cup cocoa powder
1 cup icing sugar, or more
premade espresso to taste

My French chocolate-coffee cake with green figs

Preheat the oven to 180 °C (switch on the oven fan if available). Grease a 24-cm ring cake tin.

Melt the butter, cocoa powder, castor sugar and chocolate in the microwave for about 4 minutes, stirring after each minute.

Sift the flour, baking powder and salt into a mixing bowl, then lightly whisk in the egg yolks, vanilla essence, brandy and espresso. Mix in the cocoa powder and chocolate mixture. The batter should be of a medium thickness; add more flour if it is too runny or more espresso if it is too dry.

Whisk the egg whites until stiff peaks form, then lightly fold them into the batter. Pour the batter into the prepared pan and bake for 40 minutes, or until the cake starts to pull away from the tin and a metal skewer inserted comes out clean.

In the meanwhile, make the syrup by heating the sugar, water and espresso in a saucepan over a medium heat, stirring until the syrup thickens. Remove from the heat and leave the syrup to cool slightly. Pour the syrup over the still-warm cake and leave to cool for 1–2 hours in the pan. Gently loosen the sides of the cake and turn out onto a wire wrack.

For the icing, melt the butter and chocolate in the microwave on high for about 3 minutes. Add the cocoa and mix well. Gradually add the icing sugar until the mixture reaches a spreadable consistency. Flavour with espresso to taste. Add more icing sugar if the mixture is too runny or add espresso if the mixture is too thick. Spread the icing over the whole cake.

Decorate the cake with the chocolate curls and preserved green figs. Drizzle over the fig syrup. Finally arrange the fresh fig halves, rose petals and mint leaves around the green figs.

Sift a little icing sugar over the top of the cake as a finishing touch if you like.

Makes 12

½ cup soft butter
½ cup castor sugar
3 large eggs
2½ cups cake flour
1 Tbsp baking powder
a pinch of salt
½ tsp ground cinnamon
1 cup buttermilk
1 cup finely chopped
    preserved green figs
1 cup almonds, toasted and
    chopped

Caramel topping

½ cup butter
½ cup white sugar
½ cup evaporated milk
½ tsp bicarbonate of soda

Cream cheese icing

125-g tub smooth cream
    cheese
¼ tsp vanilla essence
½ cup icing sugar, sifted
⅓–½ cup double thick cream

Cara and Kate's fig and almond cupcakes

Preheat the oven to 180 °C. Cut out squares from brightly coloured baking paper, and place two squares (crosswise in a star shape) into each cup of a 12-cup cupcake tin, or use pretty store-bought cupcake liners.

Cream the butter and castor sugar together until light and fluffy. Fold in the eggs, one at a time. Sift the dry ingredients together, then whisk into the butter mixture, alternating with the buttermilk. Mix until just combined, then fold in the figs and almonds. Pour the mixture into the paper liners, filling each about three-quarters full and bake for 20–30 minutes. Remove from the oven and leave to cool.

Combine all the ingredients for the caramel topping in a saucepan, simmer until the sugar has dissolved, then bring to the boil for about 10 minutes until golden, but do not stir. Pour the mixture into a bowl and beat until it thickens to a spreadable consistency. Spread over the tops of the cooled cupcakes.

To make the cream cheese icing, whisk the cream cheese until it is smooth and easy to spread. Add the vanilla essence and icing sugar and mix until combined. Whisk in the cream until combined, thick and smooth. Spread the cream cheese icing over the caramel topping.

The caramel icing is almost toffee-like while the velvety cream cheese icing neutralises the sweetness of the figs.

Tradouw tiramisu

Serves 8–10

¼ cup castor sugar

2 large eggs, separated

1 cup mascarpone

3 Tbsp brandy

½ cup Kahlua coffee liqueur

1 cup dried cranberries

½ cup coarsely crushed
almonds

1 cup cream

500 g lady finger (Boudoir
or Savoiardi) biscuits

1 cup strong premade
espresso, at room
temperature

80-g slab dark chocolate,
coarsely grated

3 tsp cocoa powder
for sprinkling

In a bowl, beat the sugar and egg yolks together until pale yellow. Add the mascarpone, brandy, coffee liqueur, cranberries and almonds. In another bowl, whisk the egg whites until stiff peaks form, then fold them into the mascarpone mixture.

In a separate bowl, beat the cream to soft peak stage, then fold into the mascarpone mixture.

Pack half the biscuits tightly along the bottom of a 2-litre glass dish (4–6 cm deep). Pour half the espresso evenly over the biscuits. Spread half the mascarpone mixture over the biscuits and sprinkle half the grated chocolate on top. Repeat with the remaining biscuits, espresso and mascarpone mixture, creating soft peaks on top to add texture.

Sprinkle the remaining chocolate and cocoa powder on top, cover with clingfilm and refrigerate overnight, or at least 8 hours.

Tiramisu is a heavenly Italian dessert made with espresso, lady finger biscuits, mascarpone and chocolate, but I give it a Little Karoo twist with the cranberries and almonds.

Little Karoo berry trifle

Serves 10

4 egg yolks, at room
  temperature
1 tsp vanilla essence or seeds
  of 1 vanilla pod
¼ cup honey
¾ cup castor sugar
2 cups cream
2 cups fresh cherries, pitted
  and halved
1 cup fresh gooseberries
1 cup fresh raspberries
1 cup fresh blueberries
1 cup fresh blackcurrants
2 cups chopped strawberries
2 Tbsp Cointreau
¼ cup brandy or berry juice
500 g lady finger (Boudoir or
  Savoiardi) biscuits
½ cup finely chopped
  fresh mint

Place the egg yolks, vanilla essence or seeds, honey and half a cup of the castor sugar in a large bowl. Position the bowl over a saucepan of simmering water (the base of the bowl should not touch the water). Beat the mixture until thick and creamy. Remove from the heat and continue beating for about 1 minute while the mixture cools.

In a separate bowl, beat one-and-a-half cups of the cream until soft peaks form, then fold into the egg mixture. Refrigerate the custard until cold.

Place the cherries and berries in a bowl (but keep some for decoration). Sprinkle the remaining castor sugar, Cointreau and brandy over the fruit.

Line the base of a 1.5-litre glass dish with half of the biscuits. Spoon half the fruit over the biscuits and cover with half the chilled custard. Repeat with the remaining biscuits, fruit and custard. Cover and refrigerate, preferably overnight, but at least 2 hours if time is limited.

Whisk the remaining cream until soft peaks form and decorate the trifle with the cream, reserved fruit and fresh mint.

Delicious for Christmas or Sunday lunch — use any berries you can find and adjust quantities to taste. Pick your own fresh berries in season at the Wildebraam Berry Estate outside Swellendam.

Meyer's favourite dessert

Serves 8

1 cup cream

2 x 80-g slabs dark chocolate, finely chopped

½ cup Nutella

3 large eggs, separated

¾ cup castor sugar

1½ cups milk

½ cup cake flour, sifted

1 cup freshly squeezed orange juice

3 Tbsp freshly squeezed lemon juice

grated zest of 1 orange

grated zest of 1 lemon

3 Tbsp butter, melted

2 tsp grapefruit or other citrus marmalade

Preheat the oven to 180 °C. Grease a 25-cm ovenproof dish.

In a saucepan, bring the cream to boiling point, then whisk in the chocolate and Nutella until the chocolate has melted. Pour into the prepared dish and set aside to cool.

In a bowl, beat the egg yolks and sugar until light and fluffy. Add half the milk and whisk until the sugar has dissolved.

Whisk in the flour, followed by the remaining milk. Add the orange and lemon juice and zest, melted butter and marmalade. Beat the egg whites until stiff and fold into the mixture. Spoon the mixture into the ovenproof dish, over the chocolate and Nutella mixture. Smooth the top.

Place the dish in a roasting pan with boiling water (the water should reach halfway up the sides of the dessert dish) and bake for about 45 minutes, until browned. The dessert should have a fine crust on top and a sauce at the bottom.

TIP: Serve on a cold winter's night with whipped cream and a little brandy – delicate and delectable!

My thanks to Errieda du Toit for this recipe. I've given it a twist with chocolate as well as lemons from the Tradouw Valley.

Baked Tradouw coconut, pear and berry tarts

Serves 6

Poached pears

¼ cup muscadel, or more

1 piece stick cinnamon

ground cinnamon to taste

6 ripe soft-eating white pears, peeled, cored and thinly sliced or quartered

Topping

1¼ cups cake flour

1 tsp baking powder

½ cup castor sugar

½ cup fine desiccated coconut

½ cup finely chopped almonds

4 eggs, beaten

1½ cups cream

1½ cup evaporated milk

2 tsp vanilla essence

½ cup blackberries or cranberries

1 cup canned cherries, drained (optional)

Preheat the oven to 200 °C. Thoroughly grease 6 small fluted ramekins.

To prepare the poached pears, heat the muscadel, stick and ground cinnamon in a saucepan and poach the pears until soft but not disintegrated. Add more muscadel if necessary. Set aside.

For the topping, sift the flour, baking powder and castor sugar together, then add the coconut and almonds. In a separate bowl, mix together the eggs, cream, evaporated milk and vanilla seeds or essence. Make a well in the flour mixture, pour in the egg mixture and mix to a smooth batter.

Arrange the berries, cherries and poached pears in the ramekins. Pour the batter evenly over the fruit, covering as much of it as possible. Bake for 25–30 minutes in the centre of the oven, then switch on the grill and bake for a further 5 minutes until the topping has browned slightly. Leave to cool slightly before serving.

TIP: Serve these delicious tarts with crème fraîche or whipped cream. Decorate further with fresh blackcurrants and mulberries and sift icing sugar and ground cinnamon over the top.

I always use our delicious Packham's Triumph or Bon Chrétien pears from the Tradouw Valley when making these tarts.

Macadamia, pecan nut and cranberry nougat

Makes 10 squares

2 sheets rice paper
2 cups sugar
1 cup liquid glucose
½ cup honey
¼ cup water
2 extra large egg whites
a pinch of cream of tartar
1 tsp vanilla essence
100 g macadamia nuts,
    toasted and chopped
50 g pecan nuts, toasted and
    chopped
50 g dried cranberries
cornflour for cutting and
    storing

Line the base of a 18 x 28-cm tray with rice paper.

In a saucepan, heat the sugar, glucose, honey and water over a medium heat, stirring until the sugar has dissolved. Do not allow the mixture to come to the boil before all the sugar has dissolved. Brush the sides of the saucepan with water to prevent crystals from forming. When the sugar has dissolved, increase the heat and bring the mixture to the boil. Leave to simmer for 5 minutes without stirring (if using a sugar thermometer, allow to reach 120 °C), then immediately remove from the heat.

In the meanwhile, beat the egg whites and cream of tartar together in an electric mixer until soft peaks start to form. Continue mixing on a low speed and slowly pour the sugar mixture into the egg whites. Increase the speed for about 5 minutes until the mixture cools down and starts to thicken. Gently stir in the vanilla essence, nuts and cranberries until combined.

Pour the mixture into the lined tray, pressing it down slightly. Place another sheet of rice paper over the top and leave to stand for a few hours until the nougat sets. Cut into squares with a sharp knife, dipping the knife into the cornflour if it becomes sticky. Sprinkle each square with a little cornflour. Cover the squares with wax paper and refrigerate for 3 hours before serving or wrapping.

My children buy the ingredients for this nougat with their pocket money. In turn, I buy the nougat from them to stock the deli and they make a little profit, but not, of course, if they eat it all themselves!

**Makes a 23-cm
cheesecake**

Base
¾ packet tennis biscuits
2 tsp dukkah (see page 189)
2 Tbsp butter, melted

Filling
3 x 230-g tubs full-cream
    cottage cheese
1 cup freshly squeezed
    lemon juice
1 tsp finely grated lemon zest
1 cup cream
385-g can condensed milk
4 eggs, separated
a pinch of cream of tartar
1 cup castor sugar

Alfresco Deli's lemon meringue cheesecake

Grease a 23-cm loose-bottomed baking tin.

To make the base, crush the tennis biscuits, add the dukkah and melted butter and mix together. Press the biscuit mixture over the base and sides of the tin.

Preheat the oven to 180 °C.

For the filling, mix the cottage cheese, lemon juice and zest, cream, condensed milk and egg yolks together and pour the mixture over the base.

Whisk the egg whites until soft peaks form and add the cream of tartar. Continue mixing and slowly add the sugar. Spoon the meringue on top of the condensed milk mixture and bake for 20 minutes. Switch off the oven and leave to cool in the oven for about 2 hours.

*This cheesecake isn't overly sweet, and is delicious served
with a cranberry or blackberry coulis.*

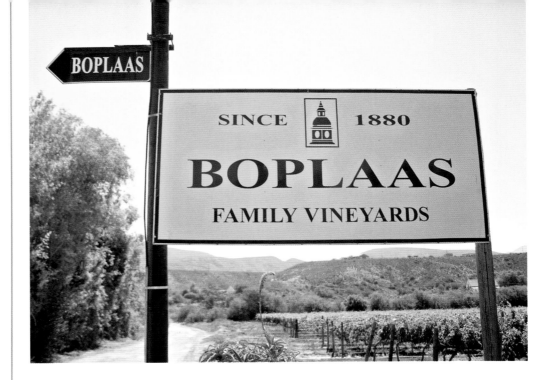

Lime soufflé

Serves 8–10

butter for greasing
4 tsp cornflour
¾ cup milk
1 vanilla pod
2 Tbsp freshly squeezed
    lime juice
2 tsp grated lime zest
4 egg yolks
6 egg whites
½ tsp coarse salt
⅓ cup castor sugar
1 cup cream
½ cup sweet sherry
finely grated lemon zest
    to taste

Preheat the oven to 180 °C.

Mix the cornflour with a little of the milk to make a smooth paste. Pour the remaining milk into a saucepan. Slice open the vanilla pod, scrape out the seeds and add them to the milk. Stir in the cornflour paste and simmer over a low heat until thickened. Keep stirring to avoid lumps.

Remove from the heat, add the lime juice, zest and egg yolks, then beat well. Whisk the egg whites with the salt until soft peaks form. Gradually add the castor sugar and beat to stiff peak stage. Mix a spoonful of the egg white mixture into the egg and lime mixture, then quickly and gently fold in the remaining egg white. Spoon into a 1.7-litre soufflé dish and bake for 30–35 minutes, or until risen and golden-brown.

Just before the end of baking time, whisk the cream until soft peaks form. Remove the soufflé from the oven and drizzle over the sherry and lemon zest while the soufflé is warm. Serve immediately with the whipped cream.

This lime-flavoured soufflé was inspired by Abigail Donnelly.

Lavender crème brûlée

Serves 6

1 vanilla pod
2 cups cream
1 piece stick cinnamon
4 large egg yolks
¾ cup castor sugar
1 Tbsp chopped lavender
flowers (no stems)

Preheat the oven to 150 °C.

Cut open the vanilla pod and scrape out the seeds. In a saucepan, simmer the seeds and pod, cream and cinnamon over a medium heat for 2–3 minutes, then remove from the heat and leave to cool for about 15 minutes. Discard the vanilla pod and cinnamon stick.

Whisk the egg yolks and a third of the sugar together until pale yellow. Pour a little of the cooled cream mixture into the egg yolk mixture and mix well, before stirring in the remaining cream. Divide the mixture evenly among 6 ramekins with a diameter of about 8 cm. Arrange the ramekins in a deep ovenproof dish, then pour hot water into the dish to reach halfway up the sides of the ramekins. Bake for about 45 minutes, or until lightly set. Leave the ramekins to cool before refrigerating for a few hours or overnight.

Melt the remaining sugar in a saucepan and simmer (without stirring) until it is caramel-like in colour. The sugar must not burn or become dark brown. Lightly grease a flat baking dish and pour the sugar mixture into it. Set aside to cool and harden into a caramel.

Once cool, break the caramel into smaller pieces. Using a grinder, grind the caramel and the lavender flowers together until fine. Spoon a layer of this mixture over the top of each ramekin.

Preheat the oven grill until hot. Arrange the ramekins on an oven tray and grill them until the caramel and lavender mixture starts to melt and is light brown. Remove from the oven and leave the caramel topping to set before serving the crème brûlées.

My Little Karoo rice pudding

Serves 6

2 cups cooked white rice
2 cups milk
½ cup coconut milk
½ cup white sugar
a pinch of salt
2 eggs, separated
2 Tbsp butter
1 tsp vanilla essence
finely grated zest of ½ lemon

Preheat the oven to 150 °C. Grease a large ovenproof dish.

In a saucepan, heat the rice, one-and-a-half cups of the milk, coconut milk, sugar and salt over a medium heat for 15–20 minutes, or until thick and creamy. Whisk the remaining milk and egg yolks together, then add to the rice mixture and cook for a further 2 minutes while stirring continuously.

Remove from the heat and stir in the butter, vanilla essence and lemon zest. Whisk the egg whites until stiff peaks form and fold into the rice mixture. Spoon into the prepared dish and bake for 30 minutes or until just set. Switch on the oven's grill for the last few minutes of the cooking time so that dark bubbles appear on the surface of the pudding.

Serve warm with thick, homemade custard.

My mom made this dessert almost every Sunday evening, using the rice that was left over from Sunday lunch. I sometimes serve it with green fig syrup and slices of wild watermelon ('makataan').

Little Karoo *koeksisters*

Syrup

2½ cups sugar

2½ cups water

1 piece stick cinnamon

1 tsp cream of tartar

1 tsp ground ginger

4 tsp rose water (optional)

1 Tbsp glycerine

Dough

4 cups cake flour, sifted

1 Tbsp baking powder

1 Tbsp sugar

½ tsp salt

1 Tbsp ground ginger

2 tsp ground aniseed

2 tsp ground cinnamon

2 eggs

1½ cups lukewarm water

¼ cup sunflower oil

2 Tbsp freshly squeezed
lemon juice

1–2 Tbsp finely grated
orange zest

2 tsp ground cardamom

oil for deep-frying

desiccated coconut for
sprinkling (optional)

First prepare the syrup. Heat the sugar, water and cinnamon in a saucepan over a medium heat until the sugar has dissolved, then simmer for about 15 minutes until syrupy. Add the cream of tartar, ginger and rose water (if using) and cook for a further 5 minutes. Stir in the glycerine just before removing the syrup from the heat – it makes the syrup glossy. Chill the syrup in the fridge or freezer.

To make the dough, mix together the flour, baking powder, sugar, salt, ginger, aniseed and cinnamon in a mixing bowl until well combined. Add the eggs, one at a time, followed by the water, oil, lemon juice, orange zest and cardamom, mixing until it becomes a soft dough. Leave to rest for 10 minutes.

Roll out the dough to a thickness of 2 cm. Use a sharp knife to cut out triangles or shapes of your choice. Remember that the dough will rise while frying, so the shapes will become bigger.

Fill a saucepan or deep fryer until half-full with oil and heat. Test the temperature of the oil by carefully dropping a small piece of dough into it; when the dough floats to the top quite quickly, the oil is ready. Deep-fry the *koeksisters* until golden-brown then drain in a sieve. Plunge the warm koeksisters into the cold syrup, remove with a slotted spoon and sprinkle with coconut if using.

TIPS: Make the *koeksisters* only once the syrup is completely chilled. The syrup must simmer for quite a while but must not change colour. Finally, when frying the *koeksisters*, the oil must be warm but not too hot, otherwise they will burn.

In summer I serve these 'koeksisters' over home-made ice cream, with fresh berries or cherries. My grateful thanks to Herman Lensing for the recipe.

Apple puffs with sabayon

Serves 4–6

freshly squeezed lemon juice
   for drizzling
5 small apples (Pink Lady or
   Sundowner), cored and
   sliced into 5-mm slices
1 cup cake flour
1 tsp baking powder
a pinch of salt
1 large egg
½ cup milk
1 Tbsp melted butter
sunflower oil for frying
1 tsp ground cinnamon
a pinch of mixed spice
¼ cup sugar

Chocolate sorbet
1 cup water
¼ cup castor sugar
2 tsp cocoa powder
⅓ cup chopped dark
   chocolate
1 tsp brandy

Sabayon
3 egg yolks
½ cup castor sugar
2½ Tbsp orange liqueur

First make the chocolate sorbet. In a small saucepan, heat the water, castor sugar and cocoa powder over a medium heat and stir until the sugar has dissolved. Bring to the boil, then reduce the heat and whisk in the chocolate until smooth. Stir in the brandy, remove from the heat and leave to cool. Freeze in shapes of your choice.

For the sabayon, add the egg yolks, castor sugar and liqueur to an aluminium bowl placed over a saucepan of boiling water. Beat continuously until light and thickened. Spoon over the apple puffs when ready to serve.

To prepare the apple puffs, drizzle the lemon juice over the apple slices to stop them from discolouring.

Sift the cake flour, baking powder and salt together. Beat the egg, milk and melted butter together, then fold this into the dry ingredients until it becomes a smooth batter.

Heat a little oil in a frying pan over a medium to high heat. When the oil is hot, dip slices of apple, a few at a time, into the batter then fry until golden-brown on both sides. Drain on paper towel.

Combine the cinnamon, mixed spice and sugar and sprinkle the mixture over the apple puffs while they are still hot.

Serve the puffs hot, topped with the sabayon, alongside the cold sorbet.

TIP: The puffs go down very well if served with milk tart shots. To make these, mix together a half cup each of vodka, condensed milk and evaporated milk. Pour into shot glasses and sprinkle ground cinnamon on top.

This dessert was inspired by http://idees.co.za/kos-onthaal. I have given the recipe my own twist by adding the sabayon and serving it with chocolate sorbet.

Beate's tarte tatin

Serves 8–10

Pastry

125 g butter, cubed
1 cup cake flour, sifted, plus
    extra for dusting
½ cup sugar
a pinch of salt
finely grated zest of 1 lemon
2 egg yolks
2 Tbsp iced water, or more

Filling

1 cup sugar
½ cup apple cider vinegar
juice of ½ lemon
seeds of 1 vanilla pod
125 g butter, cubed
6 apples (Sundowner or Pink
    Lady), peeled, cored and
    quartered
1 cup cream
1 cup mascarpone
cinnamon-sugar to taste

To prepare the pastry, line a 20-cm cake tin with clingfilm.

In the bowl of a food processor, combine the butter, flour, sugar, salt and lemon zest, pulsing until the mixture resembles fine bread crumbs. Add the egg yolks and water. Process until everything is well blended. If it looks too dry, add a little more water and continue processing. The mixture should come together in a ball.

Turn out the pastry onto a floured surface and knead until it becomes a smooth ball, then roll it out into a circle with a 30-cm diameter. Line the prepared cake tin with the pastry and refrigerate overnight (or at least 1 hour if time is limited).

For the filling, combine the sugar, apple cider vinegar, lemon juice and vanilla seeds in a non-stick ovenproof pan with a diameter of 25 cm. Bring to the boil and brush the sides of the pan occasionally with a pastry brush dipped in water to prevent crystals from forming. After 6–7 minutes, the mixture should start turning light brown. Ensure that everything cooks evenly. Cook the mixture for another minute until it is a deep orange colour. Remove from the heat and stir in the butter, about 2 blocks at a time. It will start to bubble, so be careful!

Fan the apples out, beginning in the centre, over the top of the sugar mixture. Work neatly because the current base of the filling mixture is going to end up on top. Cook over a medium heat for about another 20 minutes. Remove from the heat and leave to cool completely.

Preheat the oven to 220 °C.

Position the chilled pastry on top of the cooled pan (the pan must be cold for the pastry to cling to the sides). Tuck the pastry in, around the apples, ensuring that the edges have a thicker layer of dough. Bake in the oven for about 20–25 minutes, or until the dough is golden-brown. Leave to cool for about 15 minutes. Place a plate upside-down on top of the pastry and invert carefully so that the tart gently comes out of the pan and onto the plate. Cut it into individual slices.

Whip the cream until soft peaks form, then fold in the mascarpone and stir through the cinnamon-sugar. Decorate the tarte tatin slices with spoonfuls of the cream mixture.

Meyer enjoys the Muscat Joubert (drawn from a 115-litre vat that has been in the Joubert family for over 200 years) with this pudding! It complements the chocolate fruitiness beautifully!

Serves 8–10

6 thick slices of white bread, cubed
½ cup fresh cranberries
10 blocks dark chocolate
¼ cup toasted almond flakes
¼ cup sugar
2 Tbsp butter
4 cups milk
2 Tbsp coconut oil
1 vanilla pod, seeds scraped out
1 piece stick cinnamon
2 whole cardamom pods, bruised
3 eggs, beaten

Topping
½ cup melted butter
1 cup sugar
1 egg
1 tsp vanilla essence
¼ cup cream

Alfresco Deli's cranberry bread pudding

Preheat the oven to 180 °C.

Cover the bottom of a shallow 25-cm tart dish with the bread cubes. Scatter the cranberries, chocolate and almonds among the bread cubes and sprinkle the sugar on top.

In a saucepan, heat the butter, milk, coconut oil, vanilla pod and seeds, cinnamon and cardamom until lukewarm and the butter has melted. Remove the vanilla and cardamom pods and cinnamon stick. Whisk the eggs into the milk mixture. Pour the mixture over the bread and allow to soak in well.

Bake the pudding for about 40 minutes, until cooked and set (not too stiff, but more like a milk tart as it will continue to set as it cools).

For the topping, beat the topping ingredients together and spread evenly over the hot pudding as soon as it comes out of the oven. Return to the oven and bake for a further 20–25 minutes until nicely browned.

Serve with ice cream and good thick custard.

Pink meringue

Meringue

8 large egg whites
1 tsp red food colouring
(more if you prefer brighter
pink meringue)
2 cups castor sugar, plus
2 Tbsp extra
3 cups hulled and quartered
strawberries, plus a few
extra strawberries, hulled
and thinly sliced for
garnishing
1 cup blackberries
icing sugar for garnishing
fresh mint leaves for
garnishing

Mango mojito sauce

3 large mangoes, peeled and
sliced (keep a few slices for
garnishing)
⅓ cup white rum
3 Tbsp freshly squeezed
lemon juice
¼ cup granadilla pulp
⅓ cup castor sugar
2 Tbsp chopped fresh mint

Preheat the oven to 140 °C. Line a baking sheet with thick baking paper (or use a silicone mat).

Place the egg whites in a large mixing bowl and beat with an electric mixer until stiff peaks form. Add the food colouring and continue to beat at high speed. Gradually add the 2 cups of castor sugar and beat until the mixture is smooth and slightly stiff.

Spoon the mixture onto the prepared baking sheet or silicone mat, forming an oval with a shallow hollow in the centre and ensuring that the sides are thicker than the centre. Bake for 1 hour in the centre of the oven. Switch off the oven and leave the meringue in it to dry for a few hours.

Meanwhile, heat the strawberries, blackberries and 2 tablespoons of castor sugar in a small saucepan over a medium heat and simmer gently until the sugar has dissolved. Remove from the heat and set aside to cool.

To make the mango mojito sauce, use a hand-held blender to blend all the ingredients together until fine.

Place the meringue on a shallow platter, spoon the strawberry and blackberry mixture into the centre and drizzle over the mango mojito sauce. Decorate with the slices of strawberries, sift icing sugar over and garnish with reserved slices of mango and mint leaves.

TIPS: A little vinegar mixed into the meringue mixture will aid the setting process. Make a lemon-flavoured meringue by stirring 2 teaspoons of grated lemon zest through the meringue mixture after all the castor sugar has been added. Or make a chocolate meringue by adding 1 tablespoon of sifted cocoa powder to the meringue mixture after all the castor sugar has been added. (In either case, omit the red food colouring.) Decorate with berries in season.

Something extra

Alfresco Deli is the kitchen in which I experiment with foods of the Little Karoo. Make some of these for your pantry, or use them in combination with other dishes in the book. Many of them can be prepared ahead of time, allowing you to whip up wonderful meals if guests arrive unexpectedly. Remember to play with food and always be ready with something amazing from your kitchen!

Ostrich and chicken liver pâté with a port jelly variation

Makes 4 medium bowls

This recipe uses plenty of butter. It's a tasty spread to use over molasses bread (see page 56) or served as part of a tapas platter.

1 cup butter, plus ½ cup melted butter
4 onions, peeled and finely chopped
2 cloves garlic, peeled and finely chopped
2 tsp coarse salt
500 g ostrich and chicken livers, chopped and mixed
2 Tbsp chopped fresh thyme
2 tsp dried thyme
3 Tbsp port
a handful of fresh parsley, roughly torn
toasted sesame seeds to taste
freshly ground black pepper to taste
balsamic reduction to taste

Heat the butter in a pan and sauté the onions, garlic and salt over a medium heat until soft. Add the chopped livers and fresh and dried thyme. Fry for about 10 minutes until the livers are firm but still pale pink inside. Pour in the port and simmer gently until just absorbed. Remove from the heat and set aside to cool.

Mash the mixture to a fine texture, then spoon into bowls and pour a layer of the melted butter on top. When ready to serve, garnish with the fresh parsley and sesame seeds, grind over black pepper and drizzle over some balsamic reduction.

If you prefer, instead of melted butter, spoon a port jelly over the top of the pâté.

1 cup port
1 cup sugar
1 Tbsp gelatine powder

In a saucepan, heat the port with the sugar until the sugar has dissolved. While still hot, beat in the gelatine powder (or mix the gelatine with a little warm water, then add to the port mixture and mix well).

When the pâté has cooled, spoon the cooled, thick port mixture on top and refrigerate immediately to set.

Cream Sauce
Serves 4–6

2 Tbsp olive oil
1 medium onion, peeled and chopped
1 tsp white pepper
a little white wine to taste
1 tsp cornflour, mixed with a little water
1 cup cream, or to taste

Heat the oil in a pan and sauté the onions with the pepper. Add the wine and allow to steam gently. Add the cornflour mixture and cream, and simmer slowly until the mixture is neither too thick, nor too runny. Serve immediately with fillet or ostrich.

Pitas
Makes 10

10-g sachet instant yeast
1½ cups lukewarm water
1 tsp sugar
3 cups cake flour, sifted
1¼ tsp salt
⅓ cup canola oil for greasing

Dissolve the yeast in half a cup of lukewarm water. Add the sugar and stir until dissolved. Set aside for 10–15 minutes until the water is foamy.

Mix the flour and salt in a mixing bowl. Make a well in the centre of the flour mixture and pour in the yeast mixture. Add the remaining water and, using a wooden spoon or rubber spatula, stir to form a dough.

On a floured surface, knead the dough for 10–15 minutes until it is elastic and no longer sticky. Oil a large bowl and place the dough in the bowl. Turn the dough so that the whole surface is coated. Leave to rise in a warm place until doubled in size. Roll the dough into a thick sausage and divide into 10 pieces. Cover the pieces with a cloth and leave to stand on a floured surface for 10 minutes.

Preheat the oven to 200 °C. Position the oven shelf at the lowest point. Heat a greased baking sheet in the oven. Roll out each piece of dough into a circle, 10–15 cm in diameter and 5 mm thick. Arrange the circles on the baking sheet and bake for about 5 minutes until puffed, then turn them over and bake for a further 2 minutes. Using a spatula, press down lightly on top of each pita, then remove them from the oven. Leave to cool slightly before serving.

Puff pastry
Makes ± 600 g pastry

For this pastry to be a success, work quickly and ensure that the butter is ice-cold, or even frozen.

4 cups cake flour, sifted
1 tsp fine salt
2 egg yolks
1 cup iced water
4 tsp freshly squeezed lemon juice or brandy
450 g butter, divided into 3 parts and frozen

Mix the flour and salt. Add the egg yolks, iced water and lemon juice or brandy to the flour mixture and mix until it becomes an elastic dough. Knead for about 5 minutes until smooth, and toss it onto the work surface a few times.

Roll out the dough into a 35 x 35-cm square and grate a third of the butter over it. Fold the dough in half (creating a rectangle). Lightly score vertical lines on the rectangle, dividing it into 3 equal sections. Fold the right third over the centre third, then fold the left third over the other two thirds. Roll out again and repeat this process until all the butter has been used.

Refrigerate overnight and roll out before baking. If using the pastry for a tart or pie, line the dish with the pastry, cover with dried beans and bake blind in the oven at 230 °C in a preheated oven until golden-brown.

TIPS: Make sure that all the ingredients and utensils are cold when making this pastry. Due to the fine texture of the dough, the dough must be resilient when rolling in the butter. This is achieved by following the kneading process described above.

Shortcrust pastry
Makes enough to line a 23-cm pie dish

If I'm short of time, I use this recipe.

2 cups cake flour, sifted
½ cup cold butter
2 Tbsp iced water

Blitz the flour and butter in a food processor. Add the water to bind the dough. Wrap in clingfilm and refrigerate for 30 minutes to chill.

TIP: Roll the pastry out thinly, line a dish with it and pour a filling directly onto the pastry. There is no need for blind baking.

Sean Daniel's tagliatelle pasta
Serves 4

Sean Daniel of Magpie, in Barrydale, makes this for us!

1 cup cake flour, sifted
1 cup semolina
a pinch of salt, plus 1 tsp to cook the pasta
4 egg yolks (usually 1 egg yolk per person)
3 Tbsp canola oil

Knead the flour, semolina, pinch of salt and egg yolks together into a smooth dough. Refrigerate for 30 minutes. Roll it through a pasta roller about 10 times until really smooth. Cut the pasta into strips. Cook in a saucepan of boiling water with 1 teaspoon of salt and the oil until *al dente*.

Lavender apricot jam
Makes ± 4 cups

Serve this jam with olive ciabatta, molasses bread, vetkoek or roosterkoek with coarse salt, good-quality olive oil and balsamic reduction.

8 cups pitted and halved apricots
± 8 apricot pips (for flavour)
6 cups white sugar
½ cup freshly squeezed lemon juice
1 handful of lavender flowers
3 star anise

Heat all the ingredients in a saucepan and simmer until the sugar has dissolved. Bring to the boil until the apricots are soft. Stir occasionally, ensuring that the fruit at the bottom doesn't catch. Remove the lavender and pips, and transfer the jam into hot, sterilised jars.

Lime chutney
Makes ± 3 cups

Delicious with pork belly or fish

6 limes, thinly sliced (but unpeeled)
1 Tbsp coarse salt
2 medium onions, peeled and finely sliced
8 fresh green chillies, finely chopped
1 cup apple cider vinegar
1 tsp chilli flakes
1 tsp cardamom seeds, crushed

Sprinkle the limes with the salt and set aside for approximately 12 hours. Heat all the ingredients in a saucepan and simmer for about 45 minutes until soft and thickened. Pour the chutney into hot, sterilised jars.

Green tomato chutney
Makes ± 8 cups

The perfect complement to bobotie (see page 86)

2.5 kg green tomatoes, washed and chopped
2 cups peeled and finely chopped onions
2 small cloves garlic, peeled and finely chopped
1 Tbsp salt
2½ cups balsamic vinegar
300 g seedless sultanas
2 cups brown sugar
1 tsp mixed spice

Place the tomatoes, onions and garlic in a bowl, sprinkle with the salt and leave to stand for 1 hour. Transfer to a heavy-bottomed saucepan, pour in the vinegar and sultanas and bring to the boil. Reduce the heat and simmer until soft. Add the sugar and spice, stirring continuously until the sugar has dissolved and the chutney thickened. Pour into hot, sterilised jars.

Apple chutney
Makes about 3 cups

Classically served with pork

2 each Golden Delicious and Granny Smith apples, peeled, cored and sliced
1 onion, peeled and finely chopped
¼ cup mixed raisins and sultanas
1 fresh red chilli, finely chopped
1 tsp grated fresh ginger
½ tsp ground cinnamon
1 piece stick cinnamon
a pinch of salt
1 tsp mixed spice
2 tsp pickling spice
½ cup white sugar
½ cup apple cider vinegar
½ cup white wine vinegar

In a saucepan, gently heat the apples, onions, raisins and sultanas, chilli, ginger, both types of cinnamon, salt, mixed spice, pickling spice and sugar, stirring until the sugar has dissolved. Pour in the apple and wine vinegars and simmer for 1 hour until the apples are soft and the sauce reduced by half.

Olive tapenade
Makes ± 1½ cups

3 cups black olives, pitted and finely chopped
½–1 fresh red chilli, finely chopped
½–1 fresh green chilli, finely chopped
2 tsp peeled and finely chopped garlic
⅓ cup freshly squeezed lemon juice
¼ cup olive oil

Blend all the ingredients together with a hand-held blender until smooth. Serve with warm ciabatta (see page 55).

Hummus
Makes 2 cups

Unlike the traditional version, this hummus includes corn. It's delicious with baby beetroots, fresh herbs, chunks of feta, balsamic reduction and roasted butternut and brinjal. Whether stuffed in a pita or tortilla, or spread over ciabatta, it may be served with onion marmalade, roasted vegetables, coppa or parma ham, salami or chicken.

2 cups chickpeas, canned or dried (soaked in water overnight)
2 whole cooked mealies, kernels cut from the cob
2–4 cloves garlic, peeled and finely chopped
1 tsp ground cumin
1 tsp cayenne pepper
Maldon salt to taste
¼ cup tahini
¼ cup plain cream cheese
¼ cup finely chopped fresh coriander
2 tsp chopped sweet red or green pepper
¼ cup freshly squeezed lemon juice
1 tsp paprika
2 Tbsp olive oil

Mix all the ingredients in a food processor or with a hand-held blender until creamy. If you like, add more olive oil, lemon juice, paprika or fresh coriander to taste.

Dukkah
Makes 1½ cups

¼ cup sesame seeds
¼ cup sunflower seeds
¼ cup mixed salted nuts
¼ cup ground coriander
¼ cup ground cumin

Preheat the oven to 180 °C and line an oven tray with baking paper. Place the ingredients in a bowl and toss until thoroughly mixed. Transfer to the prepared tray and spread evenly. Lightly toast for 4–5 minutes. Remove from the oven and pour into the bowl of a food processor. Pulse until fine, but not too fine or it will turn into paste. Dukkah is especially good with beetroot, quinces and ostrich carpaccio.

Pesto with mint, herbs and cashew nuts
Makes ± 1½ cups

Pesto works with almost any dish, even salad. Grow your own basil, rocket, parsley and coriander for fresh, organic pesto.

½ cup grated Parmesan
2 Tbsp cold water
¾ cup fresh mint
1 cup fresh coriander
1 cup fresh basil
2 fresh green chillies, chopped
1 clove garlic, peeled and crushed
1 tsp ground cumin
2 Tbsp freshly squeezed lemon juice, or more to taste
finely grated zest of 1 lemon
½ tsp salt
1 tsp sugar
3 Tbsp chopped or ground cashew nuts
¼ cup pine nuts
¼ cup toasted almonds
⅓ cup olive oil

Pulse the Parmesan, water, mint, coriander, basil, chillies and garlic in a food processor. When the mixture resembles a coarse pesto, add the remaining ingredients, except the olive oil. When it resembles a thick paste, gradually add the oil and pulse until the desired consistency is reached.

Index

CONVERSION TABLE

METRIC	IMPERIAL
Millilitres	Teaspoons
2 ml	¼ tsp
3 ml	½ tsp
5 ml	1 tsp
10 ml	2 tsp
20 ml	4 tsp
Millilitres	Tablespoons
15 ml	1 Tbsp
30 ml	2 Tbsp
45 ml	3 Tbsp
Millilitres	Cups
60 ml	¼ cup
80 ml	⅓ cup
125 ml	½ cup
160 ml	⅔ cup
200 ml	¾ cup
250 ml	1 cup
375 ml	1 ½ cups
500 ml	2 cups
1 litre	4 cups

SUGGESTED WINES AND SPIRITS

WINE

Joubert-Tradauw Chardonnay

Joubert-Tradauw R62 Merlot

Joubert-Tradauw Syrah

Unplugged62 Merlot

Unplugged62 Sauvignon Blanc

FORTIFIED WINE

Boplaas port

Peter Bayly port

De Krans port

Montagu muscadel

SPIRITS

Joseph Barry brandy

Inverroche gin